THE
HOMELESS
MIND

THE HOMELESS MIND

Modernization and Consciousness

PETER L. BERGER

BRIGITTE BERGER

HANSFRIED KELLNER

Random House

New York

All rights reserved under International
and Pan-American Copyright Conventions.
Published in the United States by Random House, Inc., New York,
and simultaneously in Canada
by Random House of Canada Limited, Toronto.

Library of Congress Cataloging in Publication Data
Berger, Peter L
The homeless mind.
Includes bibliographical references.
1. Technology and civilization.   2. Civilization, Modern—1950–
I. Berger, Brigitte, joint author.
II. Kellner, Hansfried, joint author.   III. Title.
CB478.B43   90194   72–10730
ISBN 0–394–48422–3   Nov. 25, '75

Manufactured in the United States of America

9 8 7 6 5 4 3 2
First Edition

Grateful acknowledgment is made to the following
for permission to reprint material in this book:
Doubleday & Co., Inc.—"The Cathedral" from Night of My Blood
by Kofi Awoonor. Copyright © 1971 by Kofi Awoonor.
The Hogarth Press and the Translator's Literary Estate—
Two lines from "Waiting for the Barbarians" taken from
Poems, by C. P. Cavafy, translated by John Mavrogorgato.
New Directions Publishing Corp.—Four lines from "The Lament
for Ignacio Sanchez Mejias" from The Selected Poems
of Federico García Lorca, edited by Francisco Lorca and
Donald Allen, translated by Stephen Spender and J. L. Gill.
Copyright © 1955 by New Directions Publishing Corporation.
The Excursus, "On the Obsolescence of the Concept of Honor,"
by Peter L. Berger, was first printed in the European
Journal of Sociology, XI (1970), 339–347.

Preface

Innumerable pronouncements have been made about modern man and his alleged consciousness. Most of them have rested on a rather slim empirical basis, but short of some gigantic research that is unlikely to be funded these days, nothing much can be done about this. They have also suffered from a remarkable lack of theoretical clarity, and this book seeks to remedy that by approaching the problem of modern consciousness from the theoretical framework of the sociology of knowledge.

The introduction explains what this means. Part I then attempts to isolate certain crucial elements of modern consciousness and relate these to the institutional processes with which they are linked. Part II analyzes the process of modernization, that is, the diffusion of modern consciousness in what is commonly called the Third World today. Part III takes up a number of phenomena

in the advanced industrial societies that appear to be pro-
tests against modernity and that (with due apologies to
the denizens of college English departments) we have
called "demodernization." The conclusion briefly discusses
the pragmatic and political implications of the argument.

This particular sequence is logically necessary, but it
poses some difficulties for the reader. By far the most
complex sections of the book are the introduction and
Part I. The argument becomes progressively less Teutonic
in Parts II and III. We would suggest that the reader
who is less interested in our theory of modern consciousness and more in our interpretation of contemporary situations start reading at the beginning of Part II and *then*
turn to what precedes this, if he is so inclined. Fair warn-
ing should be given, however, that a number of essential
concepts and interpretations are dealt with in the Introduction and Part I.

This book can aptly be described as what German
scholars call *unabgesichert*—that is, insufficiently protected from critical attacks. We have ventured into a vast
and largely uncharted territory. We have tried to construct a comprehensive theoretical framework for exceedingly complex phenomena, and in the course of this we
have brought together phenomena that have hitherto been
studied in strict separation from each other (especially
those taken up in Parts II and III). The finished book
fills us with some trepidation. We are far from certain
about many of the propositions, and we are anxious that
our argument be understood as tentative, hypothetical,
exploratory (the reader is welcome to add any other of
the adjectives with which scholars habitually assuage
their nervousness about what they have written). All the
same, we are arrogantly self-confident about one thing:
these are the questions that must be asked. They have not

been asked very often, and even more rarely with any degree of theoretical lucidity. Needless to say, the answers are few and leave much to be desired. We hope that our attempt will be criticized—even attacked—possibly taken apart and put together again in ways we do not now envisage. We hope this, not out of some innate modesty or even out of enthusiasm for scholarly debate as such, but because we are convinced that it is high time that the questions raised here moved into the forefront of social-scientific attention.

· The book has had a considerable history. The ideas in it began to germinate during 1969, when one of the authors (for political rather than scholarly reasons) became seriously interested in problems of "development" in Latin America. Work began in earnest during a summer stay in Mexico in 1970. At that time the project was limited to what has now become Part II of the book, the problems of modernization and consciousness in the Third World. The logic of our argument compelled us to expand our scope to what it is here. What started out as a sociology-of-knowledge addendum to "development theory" has thus become a much more comprehensive treatment of modern consciousness and its adventures. We may add that for ourselves this has been quite an intellectual adventure too.

Contents

THE
HOMELESS
MIND

Introduction: The Problem of Modernity and the Sociology of Knowledge

The basic problem in dealing with the concept of modernity is no different from the problem of dealing with any other historical period or phenomenon. It can be expressed by the question: In what way is this period or phenomenon distinctive? Yet there are at least two aspects of modernity that give it a peculiar place, at least in the minds of intellectuals and very probably also in those of much wider circles of people. One is the assumption that modernity is not only distinctive from but superior to whatever preceded it. The other is the large number of individuals who presume they know authoritatively what modernity is all about. A good place to begin any serious consideration of the problem is to challenge both assumption and presumption.

The assumption of modern superiority is, of course, rooted in the idea of progress, which has dominated

Western thought since at least the eighteenth century. Whatever may be said for it, this view has no place within the frame of reference of the social scientist (or, for that matter, of any empirical science, including the science of history). Progress cannot be empirically verified. Therefore, regardless of the scientist's faith in the superiority of, say, twentieth-century New York over fifteenth-century Florence, he must suspend or bracket this faith while he is engaged qua scientist in his work, just as the sociologist of religion must bracket his belief or disbelief in the existence of God while he is studying, say, Methodist church attendance. This methodological requirement has a simple but very important consequence: modernity is to be studied as a historical phenomenon—like any other historical phenomenon. This leads to the awareness that modernity has a history, with a beginning caused by factors that (at least in principle) are empirically ascertainable and, *therefore*, is very likely to come to an end at some time in the future.

The presumption that one knows exactly what modernity is all about rests, in turn, on the deceptions of familiarity. An individual is generally ready to admit that he is ignorant of periods in the past or places on the other side of the globe. But he is much less likely to admit ignorance of his own period and his own place, especially if he is an intellectual. Everyone, of course, knows about his own society. Most of what he knows, however, is what Alfred Schutz has aptly called "recipe knowledge"—just enough to get him through his essential transactions in social life. Intellectuals have a particular variety of "recipe knowledge"; they know just enough to be able to get through their dealings with other intellectuals. There is a "recipe knowledge" for dealing with modernity in intellectual circles; the individual must be able to reproduce a small number of stock phrases and interpretative schemes, to apply them in "analysis" or "criticism" of new things that come up in discussion, and thereby to authenticate his participation in what has been collectively defined as reality in these circles. Statistically speaking, the scientific validity of this intellectuals' "recipe knowledge" is roughly random. The only safe course is to ignore it as much as one can if (for better or for worse) one moves in intellectual circles. Put simply: one must, as far as possible, examine the problem afresh.

Let us quickly say that we do not claim that our approach begins with a tabula rasa. Clearly, it does no such thing. For one thing, it has a relatively narrow focus—the sociological analysis of consciousness—and in placing this in a broader framework of interpretation (for example, in terms of the institutional order of modern society) we are forced to rely on the work of others. Our methodological caveats are thus made not in a stance of assertive self-confidence but in an attitude of (if we may coin a psychology-of-science term here) cognitive nervousness. We recommend the same nervousness to everyone else concerned with this problem. Its first fruit will be the awareness that modernity is not inexorable or inevitable, that much in it may well be due to chance, and that its processes may turn out to be reversible. The second fruit will be a sober skepticism regarding all theories of modernity—including those theories one may produce oneself.

A definition is not a theory. Yet no theoretical enterprise can get off the ground without defining its terms. Unfortunately, the matter of definition is very complex indeed in the area under consideration here. Since World War II, the social sciences have dealt with the concept of modernity and modern society mostly in connection with the processes that produce these phenomena—processes that have been called *modernization* and *development* and that have inspired a large literature.[1]

The two terms have been used synonymously and as having different meanings. Both have been used to refer to economic growth. A common distinction has been to apply the term "development" to economic growth processes and "modernization" to various socio-cultural processes concomitant with them. Sometimes the two terms have been used descriptively as objective, "value-free" terms. Often (intentionally or not) they have been used to prescribe and applaud. This usage has seemed most appropriate in connection with research geared to policy, be it the policy of national governments or of international agencies such as the United Nations. The terminological gyrations used to refer to those not yet fully blessed with "modernization" or "development" reflect this point of view. One used to speak of "backward" societies. These then came to be called "underdeveloped," and later (as an expression of optimism) "developing." Clearly, to be less than "modern" or "developed" has a stigma attached to it.

Not only the stigmatization but the terms themselves have been subjected to sharp criticism, particularly by the political left. In Latin America the concept of "development," especially as used by North American social scientists, has been decried as "developmentalism" (*desarrollismo*), which has been analyzed as an ideology designed to mask the realities of imperialism, exploitation and dependency. The real problem, in this perspective, is not that of "development" and "underdevelopment," but rather (in the words of Gunder Frank) of the "development of underdevelopment"—that is, of the relationship between exploiters and exploited. The term "modernization" has fared no better than "development" in this respect.

In recent years, however, there have been similar criticisms made by social scientists less clearly identified with the political left or with Marxist perspectives. It has been argued that the concept of "development," while still useful, should go beyond the economists' mechanical measures of growth (gross national product, per capita product and per capita income being the three major ones) to include such items as income distribution, employment and political participation. The purpose of this redefinition is clearly ethical: to prevent the term "development" from being used for a situation in which, say, the benefits of growth are limited to a small stratum, an increasing proportion of the rest of the population is unemployed and hungry, and a police state keeps the resultant turmoil under terroristic control. Generally, the effort to redefine the concept (and thus the policy goals) of "development" has been motivated by a moral concern for the human costs.

We believe that the most important question facing anyone responsible for "development" is, How much human suffering is acceptable to achieve certain economic goals? There are regimes (incidentally, both capitalist and socialist ones) that are prepared to sacrifice an entire generation or more. There are others (again, both capitalist and socialist ones) that try, as far as they can, to minimize the human costs of each step in the process. We fully share the ethical aim of those who want the social sciences to conceptualize these problems (despite the fact that we believe in a separation ad hoc between scientific analysis and moral judgment, and that we find most Marxist approaches in this area one-sided and often misleading). For this reason, we are anxious that our approach not be confused with the assumptions of *desarrollismo*.

Having said all this, there is no other option but to cut the Gordian knot and take the plunge into some definitional stance of our own. While we claim no axiomatic status for our terminology, for precisely the reasons given above (those ascribed to non-Marxist critics), *we prefer to use the term "development" politically rather than scientifically*—that is, in a context of value-oriented policy thinking rather than in supposedly value-free analysis. And the values we would like to see injected into this usage are the aforementioned ones of minimizing human costs. Since, however, this book is analytical rather than political, we have tried to avoid the term "development" in our argument.

No comparable option of avoiding the term "modernization" exists. There is an empirically available and distinctive set of phenomena customarily referred to as "modern society." And since this is a *historical* entity, there is something called "modernization"—that is, a process by which the entity "modern society" was originally created and by which it continues to be diffused. Avoidance of these terms would necessitate the employment of other less familiar terms, or the invention of neologisms, which seems of doubtful use.

"Modernization" must be seen in close relation to economic growth—more specifically, to the particular growth processes released by recent technology. Marion Levy has suggested that "modernization" be directly and simply defined as the growing ratio between inanimate and animate sources of power.[2] While we do not quite go along with this, it does draw attention to the principal cause of everything connected with modernization—transformation of the world by technology. We would prefer, however, to distinguish between the technological impact on the economy and the other processes dependent upon technology. Thus, we will discuss *modernization as the institutional concomitants of technologically induced economic growth.* This means that *there is no such thing as a "modern society" plain and simple; there are only societies more or less advanced in a continuum of modernization.*

Modernization, then, consists of the growth and diffusion of a set of institutions rooted in the transformation of the economy by means of technology. There are many such institutions, and on the basis of a broad consensus in social-scientific thought (we have been particularly influenced by Max Weber in this regard), we make the following assumptions concerning them. We ascribe principal importance to those institutions directly related to the technologized economy. Closely related to these are the political institutions associated with what we know as the modern state, particularly the institution of bureaucracy. As modernization proceeds and is diffused beyond its original territory, we see the institutions of technological production and bureaucracy, together and separately, as primary agents of social change. Following Weberian usage, we call these *primary carriers of modernization.* Related to these is a multiplicity of other institutional processes that are *secondary carriers.* Among these, we assign special importance to the contemporary city and its socio-cultural pluralism. And, as we shall see later, some of these secondary carriers can attain considerable autonomy as agents in themselves.

One word of caution: In making these definitions, we do not wish to identify ourselves with mono-causal theories of "technologism" or "economism"—that is, we do *not* assume that the relationship between the technological transformation of the economy and the gamut of modern institutions has always been a simple one of independent and dependent variables. We regard it as very likely indeed (again, we are influenced by Weber) that there are *reciprocal relations of causality* between these various entities—and that the great transformation could not have taken place without antecedent processes that were neither technological nor economic (as, for example, religious and ethical interpretations of the world). Nor do we assume such one-sided causation in the contemporary situation. While we believe that the underlying "engine" of modernization is technological/economic, we are fully aware of the multiplicity of forces *acting back* upon this "engine," and, let it be added, we do not claim to be able to provide a comprehensive theory ordering all these forces in some neat parallelogram.

Throughout the book we use the terms Third World and "advanced industrial societies." We are not happy with either. The term "Third World" first came up in the 1950's, in connection with the Bandung conference and other attempts (especially by Nehru, Sukarno and Nasser) to bring together the internationally non-aligned countries of Asia and Africa. The term now covers Latin America as well, and in addition its political connotation has changed to refer to countries deemed to be aligned *against* the United States and its allies. More recently, racial minorities within the United States have also been defined as belonging to "Third World peoples." All of this is in the realm of ideological rhetoric and has little relation to empirically significant facts. Strictly speaking, the "Third World" as a political, economic or social entity does not exist. The term is useful, however, in referring immediately and briefly to a set of societies sharing common characteristics. We have decided to use it, if only for stylistic reasons, in preference to reiterating a phrase such as "the less modernized societies of Asia, Africa and Latin America."

The term "advanced industrial societies" has a very different history. It comes out of the idea, shared by a number of Western social scientists, that *all* societies with a certain degree of technological/economic sophistication have significant common characteristics, regardless of the ideological and political differences between them. In this respect the term has overtones of the so-called "convergence theory," which holds that Western and Soviet societies are becoming increasingly similar to one another. Much can be said against these notions, and we do not wish to identify ourselves with any particular point of view in this area. But we do agree that the societies thus designated have common characteristics, just as do the societies of the "Third World," and that these characteristics are sociologically significant. So, again, we have chosen this term as against something like "the more modernized societies of North America, the Soviet Union, and Western and Eastern Europe."

Thus far we have defined and discussed modernization in terms of institutional processes—that is, processes that are experienced and analyzable as being external to the subjective consciousness of individuals. Such analysis, be it undertaken by economists, sociologists or any other group of empirical scientists, can clarify a large number of problems, but it misses a crucial dimension, the dimension of consciousness. We are convinced that a comprehensive understanding of any social reality must include this, and we regard it as our task in this book to focus on it.

In trying to accomplish this, we base ourselves on the

sociology of knowledge as it was redefined in the phenomenological approach of Alfred Schutz and subsequently
developed by Peter Berger and Thomas Luckmann.[3] It is
impossible to give an overview of this theoretical frame
of reference here. We must, however, briefly define some
of its basic principles and key terms.

Society is viewed in this perspective as a dialectic
between objective givenness and subjective meanings—
that is, as being constituted by the reciprocal interaction
of what is experienced as outside reality (specifically, the
world of institutions that confronts the individual) and
what is experienced as being within the consciousness of
the individual. Put differently, *all social reality has an
essential component of consciousness.* The *consciousness
of everyday life* is the web of meanings that allow the
individual to navigate his way through the ordinary events
and encounters of his life with others. The totality of
these meanings, which he shares with others, makes up a
particular *social life-world.*

Consciousness in this context does not refer to ideas,
theories or sophisticated constructions of meaning. The
consciousness of everyday life is, most of the time (even,
by the way, in the case of intellectuals), *pre-theoretical
consciousness.* Therefore, the sociology of knowledge must
not concern itself primarily with the analysis of theoretical consciousness like the history of ideas or the history
of philosophy, but rather with the consciousness of ordinary people as they lead their ordinary lives.

Any particular social life-world is constructed by the
meanings of those who "inhabit" it. We call these meanings *reality definitions.* Whatever people experience as
real in a given situation is the result of such definitions.
They are of different types (some, for instance, are cognitive and refer to what *is;* others are normative and refer

to what *ought to be*) and have different degrees of theoretical elaboration (as between the consciousness of the
man in the street and that of the esteemed philosopher).
What they all have in common, insofar as they are relevant to the sociology of knowledge, is that they are collectively adhered to.

For example, there are meanings attached to bodily
experiences. In many traditional societies such experiences
are defined as resulting from the intervention of super-
natural beings; in a modern society they are generally
defined in terms of biological, chemical or sometimes psychological causes. Very different realities result from these
definitions. For three successive nights, say, an individual
has a nightmare involving his deceased grandfather, who
forces him to eat large quantities of a revolting dish. The
individual in a modern society might decide that he
should desist from his new habit of eating heavy food for
supper; alternatively, he might call his psychiatrist for an
early appointment. The individual in a traditional society
is more likely to wonder just what his grandfather is trying to tell him. The two realities differ cognitively, one
includes the possibility of grandfathers coming back in
this way, the other excludes it. They also differ norma-
tively. One norm is, "You ought to live healthily"; the
other, "you ought to stay in touch with your ancestors."
Reality definitions are part of the consciousness of ordinary, barely educated or even illiterate people. They can
also, however, be elaborated in very complicated theories,
such as a biochemical theory of digestion, a psychoanalyti-
cal theory of dreams, and a cosmology in which the living
and the dead continue to interact.

A first task of the sociology of knowledge will therefore always be a systematic description of specific constellations of consciousness. And here, phenomenology

offers helpful tools. Although consciousness is a phenomenon of subjective experience, it can be objectively described because its socially significant elements are constantly being shared with others. Thus the sociology of knowledge, approaching a particular situation, will ask: What are the distinctive elements of consciousness in this situation? How do they differ from the consciousness to be found in other situations? Which elements of consciousness are essential or intrinsic, in the sense that they cannot be "thought away"? Thus it is possible to describe a consciousness that includes the assumption of communication with the dead and to point out how it differs from modern consciousness. It is also possible to ask whether this cosmology is essential for the overall constitution of a particular society (for instance, it may be an essential element in the legitimation of political power) or whether the society could be imagined as getting along without it.

Consciousness is not a random array of elements; it is organized in patterns that can be described systematically. A sociology-of-knowledge analysis will therefore try to describe specific *fields of consciousness*. Each field of consciousness is a structure constituted by the modes and contents of what is consciously experienced. Thus an entire field of consciousness will be constituted by relations with other people defined as relatives. The contents of the field are the patterns of kinship as established in a particular society ("Among my relatives are eighth cousins") as well as the concrete experiences of these patterns ("She is an eighth cousin of mine"). There are also different modes of experience relevant to the field: the individual relates to living cousins in his everyday social life, to dead ones in dreams, ecstasies or other transformations of everyday consciousness.

There is an important distinction between the *organization of knowledge* and the *cognitive style* of a particular consciousness. The first term refers to the *what*, the second to the *how* of conscious experience. For example, the fact that there is such a thing as a dead eighth cousin is part of the organization of knowledge. The fact that he can be communicated with in a state of trance is a matter of cognitive style. As we shall see later, when we are attempting to describe the consciousness that is linked to technological production, it is possible to distinguish between the relevant bodies of knowledge and the "habits" of thinking that pertain to them.

Any specific knowledge has a *background* (phenomenology calls it a *horizon*). That is, whatever is specifically known assumes a general frame of reference. Also, the discrepant reality definitions of everyday life require some sort of overall organization. In other words, the individual needs overarching reality definitions to give meaning to life as a whole. These overarching definitions are essential to hold any society together and, for that matter, to keep any particular social situation going. Together they make up an individual's or a society's *symbolic universe*. For example, my specific knowledge of eighth-cousin Mary assumes a world in which there are eighth cousins. Put differently, it assumes a general typology within which this particular item of knowledge can be placed. But there is a discrepancy between my experience of eighth-cousin Mary, who is alive, and eighth-cousin Joe, who is dead: the one experience takes place in the "broad daylight" of ordinary social life, the other in the strange context of a trance. This discrepancy is reconciled by an all-embracing (presumably religious) view of the world in which death is only a transition between two equally real states of being. This view of the world not only holds together different sectors of the individual's experience but is important for the entire fabric of institutions and patterns in the society (from the legitimation of kinship, say, to property and inheritance rights).

A further task of the sociology of knowledge is to link the structures of consciousness to particular institutions and institutional processes. In other words, the sociology of knowledge always deals with consciousness in the context of a specific social situation. For this task, phenomenology must be replaced by the more conventional tools of sociological analysis of institutions. Here we repeatedly use the concept of *carriers;* that is, we analyze specific institutions and institutional processes as the social base for specific structures of consciousness. Put differently, any kind of conciousness is plausible only in particular social circumstances. These circumstances are what we call a *plausibility structure.* For example, in the fictitious society of our previous example it is perfectly plausible to say in the morning, "I spoke with Grandfather again last night" (the *dead* grandfather, that is). Such a statement would be drastically implausible in contemporary America and would, indeed, call for immediate cognitive emergency measures ("Well, the poor fellow has finally gone over the hill") as well as practical ones ("What number do I call for a psychiatric emergency?"). Social change invariably entails change in plausibility structures. Thus, as modernization proceeds, it is very likely that communication with dead grandfathers becomes progressively less plausible.

All of the concepts we have discussed thus far are derived from the sociology of knowledge. We have, for better or for worse, coined a few new terms, three of which should be mentioned here. We use the term *carry-over* to designate any diffusion of structures of consciousness from their original institutional carriers to other contexts. Conversely, we use the term *stoppage* to designate the arresting of such diffusion. We have derived from Ivan Illich the concept of *package*, by which we mean an empirically given combination of institutional processes and clusters of consciousness. Part of our concern in what follows is to distinguish between packages that are intrinsically necessary and those that are the extrinsically caused results of historical "accidents." In other words, we are interested in which packages of modernity can be "taken apart" and which cannot be.

For example, it is probably safe to assume that people working on complicated machinery in a factory should not go into trances. The training of workers in such a factory, therefore, is likely to include the cultivation of an anti-trance attitude on the job. This may have to be done quite strenuously in a society where trances are taken for granted. Now, there is no intrinsic reason why people could not be kept off trances at work and in them when they go home. But it is possible that the anti-trance attitude may be carried over from the one social context to the other. To prevent this, the guardians of traditional culture may take countermeasures to stop the spread of the anti-trance animus. They might, say, institute special ceremonies to get factory workers back into a pro-trance state of mind when returning home from the factory town. These countermeasures would fall under our category of stoppage. They could also be described as an effort to take apart the package of factory work and anti-trance attitude. This example, by the way, is by no means as fanciful as it may appear at first.

A number of studies have dealt with modernization and "values."[4] These have generally been made within the framework of American social psychology and have had a strong behaviorist tendency in which "values" appear as one set of factors among many. For instance, scales of modernization have been constructed in which "values" were combined with other items to measure the degree of modernity. Such an approach can be very useful, particularly in relating social conduct to elements of consciousness. It gives no opportunity, however, to describe structures of consciousness "from within"—which is what we intend to do.

Our approach also differs from the "culture and personality" perspective on the problems of modernization[5] which is generally derived from American clinical psychology, with strong Freudian or neo-Freudian overtones. We acknowledge the value of this approach in providing descriptions and perhaps explanations of sections of consciousness, especially motivation. In our view, however, this is a restrictive approach to the broader problem of objective structures of consciousness and their relationship to institutions.

Finally, we must differentiate our approach from that of various Marxists[6] who analyze consciousness as "ideology" or "superstructure." They see modernization (if indeed they use the term at all) as the imposition of "infrastructures" of domination and exploitation and interpret elements of consciousness as dependent variables. Whatever may be the validity of such analyses in specific cases, this approach, too, fails to deal with objective structures of consciousness on their own terms and to recognize that consciousness as such (and not just as an appendage to "infrastructures") may be exported or imposed.

We have no interest in this book in attacking these or other approaches different from our own. Each has its validity. We consider the principal advantage of our approach to be the possibility it offers of giving descriptions of structures of consciousness "from within" and of linking these structures to the objective meanings of institutional processes given "from without."

While the sociology of knowledge provides the theoretical frame of reference for the book as a whole, there is an important methodological difference between Parts I and III on the one hand, and Part II on the other. Parts I and III deal with societies of which we have firsthand knowledge as members and participants; this has permitted us to describe structures of consciousness to which we have immediate experiential access. Part II, dealing with societies of the Third World of which we have only limited and (more important) nonparticipant experience, does not permit such a procedure; for this reason, we have been more dependent on other observers' data in this section of our argument. We think this dual methodological procedure is legitimate, but it ought to be laid on the table.

This book is an attempt to apply a particular brand of sociological theory to an empirical problem prominent in the world today. As such, it has no pragmatic or political aims. It is, however, related to such aims, both in our own minds and in terms of its intrinsic consequences. Specifically, it is related to the increasingly loud questions being asked today about *possible alternatives* to the existing forms of modernity and modernization. We shall return to this pragmatic/political concern toward the end of the book, but we wish to make a brief remark now on the logical relation between this concern and the analyses to follow.

The question of alternatives can be approached in terms of two polar opposites. Modernity may be understood as an indivisible unity, and modernization, therefore, as an inexorable destiny, in which case there are no alternatives at all. Or, modernity may be seen as a freely manipulable complex of ingredients, in which case there is a near infinity of alternatives, as the packages of modernity can be taken apart and put together in new ways at will. It seems to us that both these positions are patently untenable, and that little is gained by raising questions in these terms. The more interesting question is that of the *parameters of choice*, that is, to determine when modernity can be manipulated and when it cannot, and thus what chances may be assigned to specific alternatives. Clearly the parameters will be determined by such institutional factors as economic and political power, but the question can also be put in terms of the intrinsic relations between institutions and consciousness. The limits of what is possible are set not only by the external requirements of institutions but also, and fundamentally, by the structures of the human mind. For this reason, the relationships dealt with in the sociology of knowledge must be of great concern to anyone interested in changing existing social conditions (not least, incidentally, to the putative revolutionary).

I

Modern Consciousness

Here I want to see those men of hard voice.
Those that break horses and dominate rivers;
those men of sonorous skeleton who sing
with a mouth full of sun and flint.

—FEDERICO GARCÍA LORCA

1

Technological Production and Consciousness

Social scientists and historians have defined modernity in different ways, and they have differed in their interpretations and prognoses regarding this phenomenon. There is well-nigh universal agreement, however, on one proposition: a central feature of the modern world is technological production. We fully share in this consensus. The question we propose to discuss in this chapter is, What are the essential concomitants of technological production on the level of consciousness?

It is important to emphasize that the question concerns the everyday consciousness of ordinary people engaged in technological production. In other words, we are not concerned here with the consciousness of the engineer, let alone the physical scientist. It is particularly important to make this point in view of the fact that much discussion about modern consciousness has focused on "the scientific world view" or "the engineering mentality." There can be no doubt not only that scientists and engineers have a specific view of the world but also that this view has decisively influenced the present shape of technological society, and thus the consciousness of all of its members. All the same, the number of scientists and engineers, even in a society as modern as the American one, is very limited. A sociology of knowledge that understands itself in terms of the analysis of everyday consciousness would be ill-advised to concentrate on this small number of intellectuals. Rather, it will seek to understand the consciousness of the vastly larger number of ordinary people whose everyday lives involve them in various facets of technological production. In what follows, therefore, the reader is asked to place himself in the situation of an ordinary worker in contemporary industry. Since we intend to describe the consciousness in question very broadly, we cannot take into account obvious differences that exist between various types of technological production. Thus, we cannot take into account the differences between, say, the consciousness of a relatively unskilled worker on an automobile assembly line and that of a highly skilled technician making precision instruments. We would contend, however, that the following description refers adequately to a very broad segment of contemporary technological production.

What organization of knowledge is intrinsic to technological production?

Quite apart from the specific knowledge about technological matters that may be in the consciousness of a particular individual, that specific knowledge has a much larger background. This background contains a vast body of scientific and technological knowledge, including a body of rules for acquiring and applying this knowledge, which is present and taken for granted in the worker's everyday consciousness, although, of course, he does not *possess* this larger knowledge. In the language of phenomenology, the knowledge is deeply sedimented in his consciousness even though it cannot be thematized. Put more simply, the worker's specific knowledge derives its location and significance from this larger body of knowledge, although the latter is not available to the worker in his immediate situation. Yet while this is so, the larger body of knowledge is *potentially* available to him—or so he thinks. What he does in fact know appears to him as part of this larger body of scientific and technological knowledge, and what he in fact does in his productive activity thus becomes for him a participation, to however Lilliputian a degree, in the vast enterprise of technological production in modern society. Also, because of the rational quality of the scientific and technological body of knowledge, the worker may feel that if only he had been given certain training, he could and would be a fuller participant. In this way the impressive edifice of modern science and technology *in toto* looms on the horizon of every activity of technological production, not only as analyzed by an outside observer but in the consciousness of the ordinary worker.

An important element in the specific knowledge of the worker is the knowledge of a hierarchy of experts, which is also taken for granted and which is apprehended as being potentially available if needed. This hierarchy stretches from concrete face-to-face relationships (say, with foremen) to relationships apprehended in complete anonymity (say, with as yet unencountered experts who might intervene in the situation in some future emergency). The worker may define himself as *one* of these experts.

There is, of course, the worker's knowledge of his specific job, for which he had to be trained. At the same time he could be retrained (and may already have been) for *comparable* jobs. In other words, his work knowledge is not only one of content (though it is that too, of course, with varying degrees of complexity) but is knowledge of a *style* of work whose features can be described. The most important feature is *mechanisticity*. This means that the work process has a machinelike functionality so that the actions of the individual worker are tied in as an intrinsic part of a machine process.[1] A correlate of mechanisticity is *reproducibility*. No action within the work process is in principle unique. It can be reproduced and indeed must be reproducible, either by the same worker or by another worker with comparable training. This means that the worker's own productive activity entails *participation in a large organization* and in a *sequence of production*. The individual's own work is related to the work of many other people regardless of whether these others are physically present in the work situation (as they would be in a large factory) or not (as would be the case in a workshop producing components for use elsewhere). The individual worker's job is a step in a sequence—say, step four in a sequence of twelve steps. This sequence is apprehended and taken for granted by him as logical, even if the engineering logic behind it is not completely understandable to him. Finally, an intrinsic element of the style of work in question is *measurability*. The individual worker's job can be and is evaluated in terms of precise, probably quantifiable criteria.

What is the cognitive style intrinsic to technological production?

It is important to stress that the cognitive style is fundamentally given in the relationship of this type of work to a machine process and the logic of the latter. It is *not* necessarily present in the consciousness of the worker in terms of this logic, though this logic forms the background of his own consciousness as it pertains to the work process. In phenomenological terms, the cognitive style is not necessarily at hand in thematizable form for the worker, but it provides the background of his thematizations.

A strategic element in the cognitive style in question is *componentiality*.[2] The components of reality are self-contained units which can be brought into relation with other such units—that is, reality is *not* conceived as an ongoing flux of juncture and disjuncture of unique entities. This apprehension of reality in terms of components is essential to the reproducibility of the production process as well as to the correlation of men and machines. For example, each of several hundred cogs involved in a day's work is, given certain presuppositions (such as size), a unit freely exchangeable with every other unit, at least for the purpose at hand. Reality is ordered in terms of such components, which are apprehended *and* manipulated as atomistic units. Thus, everything is analyzable into constituent components, and everything can be taken apart and put together again in terms of these components.

From this follows the *interdependence of components and their sequences*. Again, this is required both by the reproducibility and the mechanisticity of the work process. Given the same conditions (including the same actions by the worker), the same results will be obtained. This is possible only because the components are continuously interdependent in a rational, controllable and predictable way.

A further implication of this is the *separability of means and ends*. Since reality is apprehended in terms of components which can be assembled in different ways, there is no necessary relationship between a particular sequence of componential actions and the ultimate end of these actions. To take an obvious example, a particular assemblage of cogs produced in a highly specific production sequence may eventually go into a passenger automobile or a nuclear weapon. Regardless of whether the worker involved in this particular production process approves or even knows about its intended end, he is able to perform the actions that are technologically necessary to bring it about.

Closely related to the preceding is a pervasive quality of *implicit abstraction*. Every action, however concrete, may be understood in an abstract frame of reference. Again, the example of cogs assembled in accordance with a production logic that may be divorced from any concretely imagined end may serve by way of illustration. This implicit abstraction is endemic to the technological production process. The very logic of technology demands it, even if it is not immediately or continuously present in the worker's consciousness.

All elements of knowledge in a human society are linked to specific contexts of social life and in many cases represent specific institutions. This characteristic, too, takes peculiar forms in the context of technological production Here each item of knowledge represents much larger classes of items. For example, a screw represents machines in general. It also represents, in a particular case, all of the automobile industry. Furthermore, it represents technology in general. In other words, each item of knowledge is never a concrete item and that concrete item *only*. If it should ever become that to a worker, as might happen in a moment of aesthetic contemplation, then he would be in a state of consciousness that is divorced from the production process and is probably inimical to it. To make this point one need only imagine an artistically inclined worker on an assembly line who, smitten by his muse, loses himself in contemplation of the unique and irreproducible features of a particular screw. Such contemplation would clearly be irrelevant to the performance of his job and (certainly if repeated with any degree of regularity) would eventually prevent him from performing his job.

This characteristic of items of knowledge relevant to the production process has far-reaching implications for the manner in which different sectors of his own life are represented in the consciousness of the worker. In terms of the worker's knowledge of his own life, the items of knowledge directly related to the work process represent a very specific segment of his social reality and *only* that segment. Thus, a particular type of screw and the elements of knowledge that go with it (such as knowledge of related items, knowledge of how to handle this item at work, knowledge of the sources of supply for the item and so forth) pertain to the work world of the individual and *not* to his family world. Both the specificity and the abstract character of this knowledge assign it to a segregated sphere within the consciousness of the individual. Thus the knowledge and the cognitive style pertaining to work are *segregated* from other bodies of knowledge and cognitive styles. Each of these segregated constellations of consciousness refers to specific social and institutional sectors of the individual's life. The complexity of such systems of segregated clusters of consciousness will vary with different individuals and in different social situations. Its most important and highly generalized consequence, however, is the *segregation of work from private life*. It has been frequently pointed out that such segregation *on the*

institutional level has been one of the important consequences of the industrial revolution.[3] It is very important
to understand that the same segregation pertains, and
necessarily pertains, to the *level of consciousness.*

Specific types of action in human life are related to
specific types of fantasy. The individual's actions on the
job represent larger types of action, namely, actions performed within the cognitive style of technological production. Such actions are potential projects for the individual
and therefore possible objects of his fantasy. An important
characteristic of this type of fantasy is *problem-solving
inventiveness.*[4] This type of fantasy closely relates to what
may be called a general *tinkering attitude.* Thus a certain
type of ingenuity and creativity develops which ipso facto
excludes other kinds, or at least pushes them into the
background. Despite the institutional segregation mentioned above, this ingenuity carries over to other sectors
of the individual's life. Various hobbies, particularly those
of the do-it-yourself variety, express the same features of
cognitive style in the private life of the individual, but a
problem-solving and deeply technological attitude may
also carry over into the manner in which the individual
looks at politics, the education of his children or the management of whatever psychological difficulties he may be
afflicted with.

These carry-over effects do not contradict what was
said above about the institutional segregation of work-
related knowledge. What is carried over, of course, is not
specific items of knowledge but the general cognitive style
that pertains to this type of knowledge. Indeed, the very
fact that this cognitive style is transferred, while the specific items of knowledge to which it originally pertained
are untransferable, brings out a built-in problem of modern consciousness. It is possible, for example, for the indi-

vidual to look upon his own psychic life in the same problem-solving and tinkering attitude with which an engineer contemplates the workings of a machine. However, while the engineer has a well-tested repertoire of tinkering procedures available to him for the solving of problems in the manipulation of machines, such a repertoire is sadly underdeveloped when it comes to solving problems of the human psyche. Thus it should not come as a surprise that strongly defensive reactions also exist against the carry-over of technological fantasy into other sectors of life. In private life this may take the form of an urgent quest for the "natural" as against the artificiality of the technological. Rather than tinker with more machinery in his den, a worker may then prefer to take up bird-watching as a hobby, and instead of voting for politicians who take a pragmatic problem-solving approach to public life, the worker may give his allegiance to political figures or movements of a charismatic or even anti-"technocratic" character.

Technological production brings with it *anonymous social relations*. This is not to deny the variety of concrete and sometimes rich personal relationships in the work situation—a fact pointed out by many studies of modern industry which can be very important, not only to the individual worker but to the management of the work process.[5] Nevertheless it is an intrinsic requirement of technological production that those who participate in it define each other as anonymous functionaries. If this were not done, both the mechanisticity and the reproducibility of the various components of the work process would be decisively endangered. At least in the mass-production setting of the assembly line or similar industrial contexts, social relations between workers are experienced in terms of such anonymity. The logic of the production process dictates a social experience of anonymity.[6] At the very least this introduces a dichotomy into the individual's consciousness of others: they are *both* concrete individuals *and* anonymous functionaries. Thus the worker who is in charge of step twelve in a work sequence in which I am concerned with step eleven is *both* my friend Joe, an individual with unique and irreplaceable qualities, *and* an anonymous functionary who could be replaced at any moment. At most, *all* the others in the work situation may be experienced in an anonymous mode, in which case the situation becomes anomic in the full sense of the word.

Put differently, a double consciousness develops in which the other is simultaneously experienced in terms of his concrete individuality *and* in terms of the highly abstract complexes of action within which he functions. In order for such actions to be performed, the other *must* be anonymized. Because of the imperative of anonymity, certain concretizations in the relation with others constitute threats to the production process—for example, "I'll only work with my friends," or "I refuse to work with Polacks." The production process therefore necessitates "human engineering," that is, the technological management of social relations. Although this management may involve attention to highly personal idiosyncrasies of individual workers and may even contain a positively therapeutic dimension, its fundamental purpose is to control the unfortunate intrusions of concrete humanity into the anonymous work process. Individuals become organized in accordance with the requirements of technological production. Further, in terms of the organization of knowledge, the other is defined as a carrier of specific expertise, and he derives status from this.

Once again, there may be defensive reactions against this anonymization of social relations, not only in the worker's total social existence but within the work situation itself. Some of these reactions are institutionalized, as for instance, by labor unions. Yet the same anonymity of social experience allows the worker to identify with large groups of people and sectors of society such as "organized labor," "the working class" and the like. These larger identifications are important not only politically but in terms of potential mobility within the social system.[7] Conversely, an incapacity to transcend face-to-face concrete relations with others (such as those of friendship, family or neighborhood) are hindrances due not only to participation in this type of production but also to participation and social mobility on a larger social scale.

Through the reciprocity of perspectives endemic to human social life, all these features of the experience of others also apply to the experience of self. More than that, the very anonymity of the aforementioned social experience carries over more easily to the experience of self than to highly concretized relations with others. For example, I can become a "worker" in my own consciousness much more easily than I can identify with individuals who have, say, a very peculiar sense of humor. There then occurs a process of *self-anonymization* to a high degree.[8] The self is now experienced in a partial and segmented way. Indeed, it becomes a *componential self*. A fundamental feature of componentiality intrinsic to the process of technological production is thus carried not only into the area of social relations but also into the intra-subjective area in which the individual defines and experiences his own identity.

Put differently, the componentiality of the cognitive style pertaining to technological production extends to identity. Again, a specific kind of double consciousness develops. In this case the dichotomy is between concrete identity and anonymous identity. The individual now becomes capable of experiencing *himself* in a double way: as a unique individual rich in concrete qualities *and* as an anonymous functionary. This dichotomization in the subjective experience of identity makes it possible for the individual to establish subjective distance vis-à-vis certain features of this identity.[9]

For example, the individual will now experience that portion of his identity that contains his anonymization as a "worker" as being "less real" than his identity as a private person or a family man. Since each portion of identity relates to specific roles, it now becomes possible for the individual to perform some of these roles "tongue in cheek." The componentiality of identity, as the componentiality of social relations, makes possible an "engineering" practice. This time what is involved is the "engineering" of one's own self. Those aspects of identity that are defined as "more real" must be protected against threats coming from the "less real" components of identity. Very importantly, a psychological management of considerable complexity is necessary in order to perform actions "tongue in cheek." This is a precarious business—effort-consuming, requiring a lot of thought and intrinsically unstable. In extreme cases the individual in this situation will experience "alienation," that is, he will no longer be able to recognize himself in this *or* the other component of his subjective identity. In the common usage of the notion of alienation only one type of such nonrecognition has been stressed: the case where the individual can no longer recognize himself in his *anonymized* identity. It is important to stress that the other type is just as possible, that is, the individual may feel alienated from precisely those components of his self that are *not* anonymized.[10] While the individual may seek psychological refuge from the alienations of his work situation in private life, it is also possible that an individual may seek such refuge in the very anonymity of his work situation because he finds the non-anonymous relations of private life intolerable. At the least, there will be a problem of correlating work identity with other components of identity. The macro-social implication of this dichotomy in the experience of self is this: there *must* be a private world in which the individual can express those elements of subjective identity which must be denied in the work situation. The alternative to this would be the transformation of individuals into mechanical robots, not only in the external performance of roles but on the subjective level of their own consciousness of self. Such a transformation, the extreme case of alienation, is almost certainly impossible empirically because of deep-seated features in the constitution of man.

An important feature of psychological "engineering" is *emotional management*. The logic of the production process dictates control over free-flowing emotionality. It requires and indeed institutionalizes a specific mode of emotionality. Its characteristics are that it is low keyed, "cool," controlled (in psychoanalytic terms, highly "repressed"). The work situation does indeed permit "niches" for freer forms of emotionality. Individuals may call each other by emotionally charged nicknames. They may engage in joking or playfulness and the like. These freer emotional forms, however, must always remain within the requirements of appropriate work attitudes or "morale." The implication of this is a cleavage in the emotional economy of the individual. This cleavage produces anxiety; it may produce more severe psychological disturbance. To reduce anxiety and to avert more severe disturbances a management of the emotions develops. Externally this is effected by procedures and agencies set up by those who manage technological production (including explicitly therapeutic procedures and agencies). Internally the same management is performed by the individual himself. It is clear that such management of the emotions requires considerable effort, almost inevitably runs into problems, and by its very nature is always precarious. It not only affects the individual's psychic life but even his organism. Thus highly rational structures (for example, time rhythms or functionally efficient figures of physical motion) are imposed upon the organism. There emerges a "second nature" which has a fragile and conflict-prone relation to the "first nature" of the individual. Once more, the former affects the latter in a variety of ways, ranging from the emotional control deemed necessary to achieve certain sexual results to similar controls built into the functionality of the political process.[11]

Another feature of the cognitive style of technological production may be termed the *assumption of maximalization*. For both technological and economic reasons the logic of the production process always tends toward a maximalization of results—more product for less expenditure. There is therefore a built-in innovative tendency describable, as the case may be, in terms of "bigger and better," "more and more cheaply," "stronger and faster," and so on. This assumption of maximalization enters into not only the worker's actions but his fantasy. It thus has an important carry-over potential for other sectors of his social life.

One of the important characteristics of technological production is that from the point of view of the individual "many things are going on at the same time." This is true both of the production process itself and of the multifold social processes that are connected with it. The individual must keep in touch with all of these. His relations both with material objects and other persons become very complex. To keep up with this complexity necessitates a particular tension of consciousness characterized by a quick alertness to ever-changing constellations of phenomena. This feature, an important element in the cognitive style in question, we would term *multi-relationality*.

The production process itself derives its meaning from a multi-relational context. The meaning of the process from the point of view of its functionality is always long-range. Each unit within it derives its complete meaning from the whole. This has an important consequence from the point of view of the worker: it may become difficult to ascribe meaning to *his* units within the process *unless* he has some view of the process as a whole. Typically, however, he has no such view, and the end product is not available to him in any concrete experience. At the same time, because he has been socialized into the reality of the production process, he has some sense, however vague, that he *ought* to have a view of the whole. Thus his own experience is apprehended by him as incomplete, as somehow defective. He may devise strategies to get around this, strategies expressed in statements such as "This is not my problem," or "I take it easy and let *them* worry about the big picture," and the like. These strategies are likely to have precarious results. Therefore there is a constant threat in the situation of meaninglessness, disidentification and experiences of anomie.

This threat can again be dealt with to a degree by "engineering" on the part of management. For example, the availability of the "big picture" may be conveyed by means of one kind or another of managerial ideology, such as a vision of the American productive miracle or, alternatively, a vision of the toil of the present finding fulfillment in a socialist future. All these visions, however, depend upon ongoing propagandistic efforts and are always endangered by the concrete presence of a very different experience. The threat of meaninglessness is probably a constant in this situation.

It is important to point out that the preceding refers to discontents that are endemic to work under the conditions of technological production. There are also discontents that are brought into the situation by extrinsic agencies such as the mass media, political influences (say, by labor unions), books written by intellectuals, and so on. As a result of these the worker may feel "alienated" because he does not own the means of production, or he may feel deprived because his "needs" for ongoing personal fulfillment are not met on the job, or the like. It is important to understand that such discontents are *added to* the work situation but are not essential to it. They may or may not endanger the continuing function of the production process depending on how far the latter can maintain its autonomy, that is, autonomy with regard to the subjective consciousness of those who work in it. In other words, technological production may go on for a long time even if those who participate in it feel frustrated in one way or another. The aforementioned techniques of psychological management may actually promote such a state of affairs. On the other hand, a point may be reached where these psychological tensions could endanger the work process itself. Needless to say, these additive discontents can be very real, both in the consciousness of the worker and in actual social-economic consequences. As far as the worker is concerned, they may even produce psychopathological reactions. All the same, it is important to keep them apart from the *intrinsic* threat of meaninglessness that was discussed before. Indeed, the procedure employed here is designed to separate intrinsic from additive elements in the consciousness pertaining to this type of production process.[12]

We have tried to describe a number of features of consciousness that appear to us to be essential or intrinsic to the process of technological production—that is, we find it very difficult to "think away" these elements while assuming that technological production will continue. It is clear that technological production in any given situation will contain many other elements of consciousness which could very well be "thought away." In any given situation, then, the usefulness of our procedure will be demonstrated to the extent that it makes possible a differentiation between those elements that may be "thought away" and those that cannot.

We have already had occasion to point to carry-over effects beyond the actual social area of work. We have described how elements of consciousness that are intrinsic to technological production are transposed to areas of social life that are not directly connected with such production (for example, problem-solving ingenuity). In so-called developed or advanced industrial societies, in which technological production provides the economic foundation of society as a whole, these carry-over effects are massive. Everyday life in just about every one of its sectors is ongoingly bombarded, not only with material objects and processes derived from technological production but with clusters of consciousness originating within the latter. Thus many of the above-named themes serve as contributions to an overarching symbolic universe peculiar to modernity. It is especially important to understand this, since the majority of the population is never directly engaged in technological production. For better or for worse, it is not necessary to be engaged in technological work in order to think technologically.

It is possible, then, to differentiate between *primary and secondary carriers* of these constellations of consciousness. The primary carriers are those processes and institutions that are directly concerned with technological production. The secondary carriers are processes and institutions that are not themselves concerned with such production but that serve as transmitting agencies for the consciousness derived from this source. The institutions of mass education and mass communication generally may be seen as the most important of these secondary carriers. Through school curricula, motion pictures and television, advertising of all sorts, and so on, the population is continuously bombarded with ideas, imagery and models of conduct that are intrinsically connected with technological production. As a result of this wide diffusion, some of these themes become independent of the primary carriers. These themes then become incorporated in a modern world view diffused through a multiplicity of channels which in its fully developed form is no longer dependent upon any direct connection with the actual processes of technological production. Like other fully developed world views, the world view of modernity takes on a dynamic of its own. Not only is it no longer directly dependent upon specific institutional processes, but it can itself influence or even generate such processes.[13]

Bureaucracy and Consciousness

Both technological production and bureaucracy are key phenomena of modernity.[1] There is, however, an important difference between them. Bureaucracy, unlike technology, is *not* intrinsic to a particular goal. If one has set oneself the goal of producing automobiles, there is no way of doing so except through processes of technological production. If, however, one has made the decision that citizens traveling outside the country must obtain a passport, one may set up *either* bureaucratic processes *or* nonbureaucratic ones as the means by which these passports are to be obtained. Therefore, before any further statements are made concerning bureaucracy it is possible to say: The relationship of this phenomenon to whatever sectors of social life are dominated by it has a lesser quality of necessity than the relationship of technological production to its appropriate social activities. In other words, a crucial difference between technological production and bureaucracy lies in the *arbitrariness* by which bureaucratic processes are superimposed upon this or that segment of social life.

The fundamental logic of technological production, on the level both of praxis and of consciousness, is one of productivity. This is not necessarily the case with bureaucracy. Determinants other than those of productivity shape bureaucratic processes. As a result, these have a greater degree of variability than is possible in the area of technological production. Indeed, the degree of this variability depends upon how pressing are the concerns of productivity or efficiency or comparable "engineering" considerations in the functioning of the particular bureaucracy in question. If such considerations do indeed prevail, then the particular bureaucracy entails knowledge and procedures that are very similar to those pertaining to technological production as they were described in the preceding chapter. This, of course, is especially true of bureaucracies that directly administer such production. Large-scale technological production almost invariably entails bureaucratic agencies of administration. These agencies, both in their organization of knowledge and in their cognitive style, tend to be very similar to what was described in the preceding chapter. For this reason we shall concern ourselves here with a different type of bureaucracy—to wit, political bureaucracy. In political bureaucracy there is less pressure from the logic of technology and therefore more of a chance for the peculiar "genius" of bureaucracy to unfold.

For reasons we have explained, we concentrated in the preceding chapter *not* on the consciousness of engineers or scientists but on that of the ordinary worker engaged in technological production. For similar reasons we will concentrate here not on the consciousness of bureaucrats but rather on that of their clients. In what follows, then, the reader is asked to put himself in the position of a typical client of an agency of political bureaucracy. For example, he may think of a citizen applying for a passport from the appropriate government office.

What is the organization of knowledge brought to such an encounter with bureaucracy?

In the background is the knowledge of a vast bureaucratic system of which this particular agency (say, the passport agency) is a particular instance. The knowledge of this bureaucratic universe is shared by all adults in the society. Furthermore, it may be taken for granted that any individual confronting this particular bureaucratic agency, even if he is encountering it for the first time, has had plentiful experience with similar agencies in the past. Part of this background knowledge is the generally accepted assumption that such a bureaucratic system is necessary, especially in the public/political sphere. Moreover, there is the generally accepted assumption that different areas of life are under different bureaucratic jurisdictions, each jurisdiction referring to a different institution (such as the state, the educational system or private enterprise) or to a different section of such an institution (such as different government agencies, the military or the post office). Every jurisdiction is typically taken for granted, though specific legitimations are available for each. The knowledge of these jurisdictions and their appropriate legitimations is widely distributed in society.

A key notion in the individual's knowledge of the bureaucratic system is that of *competence:* each jurisdiction and each agency within it is competent *only* for its assigned sphere of life and is supposed to have expert knowledge appropriate to this sphere. The knowledge of at least a certain range of these competences and of their boundaries is also widely distributed. Thus the individual knows where to go for a particular request. He knows the difference between the bureaucracy of the federal government and that of the local university and is therefore unlikely to seek a passport in the university registrar's office. Also, he will probably know at least some of the major jurisdictions within the federal bureaucracy and their respective competences and therefore will hardly attempt to obtain his passport from the nearest office of the Veterans Administration. There is also the knowledge that, in principle, information about these jurisdictions may be obtained if it is not in the individual's possession already. This involves the notion of *referral*, which is a key bureaucratic category. In the life of the typical bureaucrat hardly a day goes by in which he does not repeat many times the sentence "I am not competent to deal with this matter" either to other bureaucrats or to clients. The typical sequel of such a pronouncement is that the matter is referred to some other bureaucrat who *is* competent. Needless to say, these procedures of referral may be complex and very time-consuming in large bureaucratic establishments. Nevertheless there is the assumption that in the end the client will be referred to someone who is bureaucratically competent to handle his case. It follows that within the particular bureaucratic sphere "nothing is left out" from this web of competences. This is the basic bureaucratic notion of *coverage*. Thus a typical bureaucracy keeps extending its procedural rules (even if not its staff) as cases appear that have not previously been covered. Bureaucratic competences have a built-in tendency to multiply. As the files grow, so do the standard operating procedures. The suspicion that some new case may *not* be covered typically produces anxieties on the part of both bureaucrats and clients. In the extreme case (which mercifully in all likelihood is improbable in fact) this would entail the expectation that there must be an appropriate government agency to deal with every conceivable problem of individual life. But in the much less extreme case of the passport seeker there is the expectation that, however peculiar may be the conditions under which this particular individual seeks a passport, there will be the competence to handle the case somewhere within the bureaucratic procedures of the passport agency.

Another general notion about bureaucracy is that of *proper procedure*. Bureaucracy is assumed to operate within rational rules and sequences. These are known or in principle knowable. In the political sphere that most concerns us here this is, of course, directly related to the idea of legality and lawful procedure. There are laws providing for the existence of a particular bureaucracy and for many of its procedures. The very existence of the bureaucracy is legitimated by this legality, and it is assumed that the bureaucracy will operate in accordance with the law. This implies the possibility of improper procedure and of *avenues of redress*. Indeed, very often the laws that set up a particular bureaucratic agency provide such avenues explicitly. Thus an individual who deems that a passport has been denied him improperly may resort to various avenues of redress, either within or outside the particular bureaucratic agency. There are procedures of appeal and of hearings set up by the passport agency itself. There is also recourse to the courts. There are specific individuals, such as lawyers or congressmen, who are regarded as experts, to assist the individual seeking redress. Generally there is a knowledge of rights and duties which are defined in very specific (and ipso facto limited) ways. Thus the individual has the right to obtain a passport but not to obtain a diplomatic passport. He has a duty to state truthfully his dates of birth or naturalization, but not his income, on his passport application. The passport agency may ask him to tell which countries he intends to visit but not what his political beliefs are and so on. It is assumed that both rights and duties can always be translated into specific bureaucratic procedures—as long, of course, as they remain within the competence of the bureaucratic agency in question.

There is finally a general notion of *anonymity*. Bureaucratic competences, procedures, rights and duties are *not* attached to concrete individuals *but* to holders and clients of bureaucratic offices. Thus the individual's right to a passport is vested in his (bureaucratically defined) citizenship. The duty of the passport official to issue him a passport is vested in his (bureaucratically defined) office. All individual characteristics, peculiarities or eccentricities of both the bureaucrat and his client are irrelevant in principle to the business at hand and are carefully excluded from consideration by the bureaucratic procedures being enacted. What is more, any breach of this anonymity through the intrusion of concrete individuality is defined as not only irrelevant but *corrupt*. Within the bureaucratic frame of reference, corruption is any breach in this overriding principle of anonymity. Typically, where such corruption actually occurs, both bureaucrat and client tend to camouflage it by reference to anonymous interpretations of what has occurred. Thus a passport may in fact be denied because a bribe has not been offered, but the denial will be legitimated in terms of an irregularity on the passport application; or a diplomatic passport may be issued to an individual who is somebody's cousin, but this act will be explained by ascribing to the applicant some quasi-diplomatic status not readily visible to the

naked eye. In both examples, motives of concrete individuality are translated into the anonymous terms deemed
appropriate for the bureaucratic universe of discourse.
Actually, it is not concrete individuals but abstract categories that interact in the bureaucratic process. The bureaucrat is not concerned with the individual in the flesh
before him but with his "file." Thus bureaucracy is an
autonomous world of "papers in motion," or at least it is
so in principle. Naturally this principle is frequently vio-
lated as bureaucratic anonymity is ongoingly disturbed
by eruptions of concrete humanity. At the same time the
controlling and corrective power of the principle is part
and parcel of the empirical reality of most bureaucracies.
Even where this is less the case, the power of the principle
continues to manifest itself in the compulsion to give at
least lip service to it.

Thus a specific body of knowledge emerges (and with
it a specific language) which appertains to bureaucracy
and to bureaucracy only. This is segregated from other
bodies of knowledge, such as those pertaining to technological production or to private life. Bureaucracy is encountered by the individual as a highly specific social
reality. At the same time there is the possibility of carry-
over processes, both *from* and *to* bureaucracy. On the
one hand there is, for example, the bureaucratization of
personal life. Although there are few, if any, hard data
on this, we may assume that this phenomenon is most
intense among bureaucrats themselves. In any case, there
are individuals in different occupations who try to organize their households and families as far as possible along
the same lines as those of a bureaucratic office. A graphic
illustration of this is the bulletin board hung in the
kitchen or near a telephone in many middle-class American families with the express purpose of allowing

family members to write memoranda to each other or to themselves. It is not uncommon to see posted on such bulletin boards standard operating procedures (say, for getting the family shopping done or for getting ready for a party) that would reflect favorably on the management of a medium-sized office.

Conversely, there is the phenomenon of the personalization of bureaucracy. Sincerely or insincerely as the case may be, there is a deliberate effort to introduce patterns of emotionality and personal relationship into the anonymous structure of a bureaucratic agency. From the office Christmas party to the erotic by-play around the water fountain, this constitutes an attempt to incorporate elements of private life into the social relations of bureaucracy. Where such efforts are part of deliberate management policy, this is a phenomenon very similar to the "human relations" in industry that we referred to in the preceding chapter. Furthermore the body of knowledge pertaining to bureaucracy includes knowledge of at least some empirical carry-over possibilities. For example, the individual knows where he can use "personal influence." This indicates that the personalized interruptions of bureaucratic anonymity may themselves be patterned—indeed in the extreme and ironic case they may themselves be bureaucratized, as, for example, in the file kept by a politician about the personal favors owed him by various members of a bureaucratic establishment. Different bureaucracies vary considerably in the way in which personalism and anonymity relate to each other, and indeed knowledge of the particular relation is an important part of the client's knowledge about bureaucracy. A good deal of anxiety is connected with this. After all, the individual may make a mistake. This knowledge must include knowledge of differential access to bureaucracy. For example, an individual may know that he has no personal "in" with regard to a particular bureaucratic agency, but he also knows that his friend X does. This type of knowledge may itself become the foundation of a particular and often highly sought-after expertise. This expertise is represented by the role of the "fixer," often a key role in the social reality of bureaucracy.

What is the cognitive style of bureaucratic consciousness?

An overriding element is *orderliness*. Every bureaucracy must produce a system of categories into which everything within a certain jurisdiction can fit and in terms of which everything can be handled. There must be clear and concise definitions of every relevant phenomenon or situation. As bureaucratic administration continues over a period of time this system of categories expands. Bureaucracy is not only orderly but orderly in an imperialistic mode. There is a bureaucratic demiurge who views the universe as dumb chaos waiting to be brought into the redeeming order of bureaucratic administration. More specifically, this orderliness is based on a *taxonomic propensity*. This also brings about a sort of componentiality, but of a more concrete and artificial sort than that discussed in the technological sphere. Phenomena are classified rather than analyzed or synthesized. The engineer puts phenomena into little categorial boxes in order to take them apart further or to put them together in larger wholes. By contrast, the bureaucrat is typically satisfied once everything has been put in its proper box. Thus bureaucracy leads to a type of problem-solving different from that for technological production. It is less conducive to creative fantasy, and it is fixating rather than innovating. It produces a general taxonomic style which, as we have seen before, may be carried over successfully into other spheres of social life.

Bureaucracy presupposes *general and autonomous organizability*. In principle everything is organizable in bureaucratic terms. Because of its abstract formality, bureaucracy is applicable in principle to just about any human phenomenon. In the technological sphere, social organization is largely heteronomous, that is, it must be so shaped as to conform to the nonbureaucratic requirements of production. This imposes certain limits on organization. Bureaucratic agencies within the ambience of technological production are controlled by such limits. In the political sphere, which is the bureaucratic sphere par excellence, these limits are much less in evidence. Here, organization can be set up autonomously, that is, as following no logic but its own. In the extreme case, a bureaucracy may do nothing but operate *itself* (experience with bureaucracies make one wonder whether this case is really all that extreme). As a result, the processes of bureaucratic organization have a high degree of arbitrariness. This may be seen, for example, in the steps that are set up for a particular bureaucratic process and the timetables within which these steps take place. In technological production the sequence of steps is dominated by the engineering necessities in question, and these necessities set the parameters within which arbitrary variation is possible. The same is true of the timetables of production. Bureaucracy does not suffer from such handicaps. Paper does not resist the bureaucrat in the way that steel parts resist the engineer. Thus there is nothing that intrinsically prohibits the passport agency from deciding that ten rather than three bureaucrats must approve every passport application and that therefore the timetable for obtaining a passport is greatly extended.

There is a general assumption of *predictability*. It is assumed that bureaucracy will operate with certain regular procedures. These procedures are known and can therefore be predicted. This is different from the predictability of technological production, because there is much more leeway for arbitrary definitions of bureaucratic procedures. This, of course, is directly related to what has just been said about the material controls imposed upon the engineer and about their absence in the case of the bureaucrat. The arbitrariness of bureaucracy, however, has pragmatic political limits. For example, there is no technical reason why the passport office should not be open from midnight to 3 A.M. Such an arbitrary decision, however, would run into severe pragmatic difficulties and probably would have very negative political consequences for the bureaucrat making the decision. These political controls enhance the predictability of bureaucracy. There is also a carry-over of predictability from one bureaucratic agency to another. Thus, while this may be the individual's first experience with the passport agency, he has a general idea of what to expect because of his experience with other government agencies. He knows that he must fill out certain forms. He has at least a general idea of what information will be required. He is familiar with the social etiquette of government offices. He knows that his application will be processed in certain stages and so on.

There is a *general expectation of justice*. It is expected that everyone in the relevant category—as, for example, those entitled by law to a passport—will receive equal treatment. It is, of course, understood that certain persons may be excluded from this relevant category—for example, resident aliens or convicted criminals. It is also understood that the bureaucratic procedures may codify certain preferences, for example, in favor of diplomats or other people traveling on urgent government business. Once the categorial system has been established, however, the presumption of equality holds within each category. In the most general way, bureaucracy is expected to conform to the Roman principle *suum cuique*. An implication of this is that there will be no favoritism or any other intrusion of personal bias in the bureaucrat's handling of each client's case. The bureaucrat is expected to handle every case *sine ira et studio*. In other words, there is the general expectation that bureaucracy will operate impersonally and with "affective neutrality."[2] These considerations bring us to an important point: unlike anything discussed in the preceding chapter, the cognitive style of bureaucracy contains a *moral* quality, not just as a limiting factor (after all, there are also moral assumptions about technological production—for example, that no one will be killed in the course of it), but as an intrinsic part of its own structure of consciousness. The source for this moral element is probably to be sought in the primary social location of bureaucracy in the political sphere.

What emerges from the combination of the aforementioned elements of cognitive style might be described as *moralized anonymity*. In some ways this is similar to the anonymity of technological production, but here it becomes morally "charged," that is, anonymity is not only recognized as a pragmatic necessity but is given allegiance as a moral imperative. In technological production, anonymity is imposed on social experience by the extrinsic requirements of the production process. In bureaucracy, anonymity is intrinsically defined and morally legitimated as a principle of social relations. Thus the presumption of equality (that is, of anonymity in a moral sense) among all in a relevant bureaucratic category is not a technical requirement but an axiom of bureaucratic ethics. The bureaucratic system as a whole is deemed to have moral obligations toward its anonymous clientele. This indeed is the basis of the bureaucracy's legitimacy. A bureaucratic agency will be judged in terms of how well it is doing its job in this moral/anonymous way. Conversely, violations of this anonymity are subject to moral censure. Typically, a bureaucracy or bureaucratic agency will acknowledge this morality by providing regular avenues of redress.

Bureaucracy posits the *non-separability of means and ends*. Here is an element of cognitive style that is directly contradictory to that of technological production. In bureaucracy the means are typically as important, or nearly so, as the ends. It is not just a question of getting somebody a passport but of getting it to him by the proper means. And indeed this principle, too, is heavily "charged" morally. The proper means and procedures are given a positive moral value, and in many cases it is assumed that even if the legitimate end is obtained by illegitimate means, the damage done by this to the integrity of the bureaucratic agency far outweighs any positive benefits from the action. The bureaucrat will therefore always try to maintain a non-separability of means and ends because this non-separability serves to legitimate his procedures. Bureaucracy is by the same token singularly susceptible to "goal displacement."[3] This prevails when interest in the means has actually replaced the original interest in the ends and the bureaucracy concentrates all its energies on the perfection of its procedures. The purpose of the bureaucracy is now no longer to issue passports but to perfect the procedures operating within the passport agency. For pragmatic reasons it is likely that passports will still

be issued as a sort of fringe benefit to the properly bureaucratic work of art, but the focus of interest will be elsewhere. Such a situation, needless to say, will always be
profoundly galling to the client who senses that his own
problem is purely incidental from the point of view of the
bureaucrat. One may even suppose that there is a built-in
utopianism in bureaucracy which projects the perfect situation in which bureaucracy operates with no clients
whatsoever. In the vast organization of the modern state
there are bureaucracies which closely approximate such a
platonic heaven. In most instances, however, there will be
pragmatic political limits to such utopianism. Leaving
aside these idealistic aberrations, clients as well as bureaucrats typically recognize the moral character of the non-
separability of means and ends, and in many cases the
clients too have a strong moral investment in the expectation that their cases will be handled "properly."

This brings us once more to an important aspect of
consciousness in modern society that we have encountered
before in a slightly different context: the differentiation
between structures of consciousness pertaining to different
institutional spheres. Thus most individuals in contemporary society directly or indirectly encounter both the
spheres of technological production and of bureaucracy.
Differentiated structures of consciousness pertain to each.
The individual who must relate to these different institutional spheres must therefore learn to operate with different cognitive styles at different times. The differentiation
is given in the organization of knowledge and in the several cognitive styles available to him in his everyday life.
In the concrete example at hand, the individual must
know when to apply the principle of separability of means
and ends and when to apply the contrary principle of
non-separability. Objectively this difference between these

two institutional spheres has historical roots and is probably to be sought in the time differential between the developments of, respectively, bureaucracy and technological production in Western society. Be this as it may, the differentiation in consciousness is a correlate of these objective institutional developments.

The encounter with bureaucracy takes place in a mode of *explicit abstraction*. In the discussion of technological production, abstraction was seen to be implied but not necessarily available to the consciousness of the individual engaged in such production at any given moment. By contrast, the abstractness of bureaucracy is typically available to the consciousness of its client (and of course to its practitioner). In other words, there is a general knowledge of the abstract modalities of bureaucracy and at least a very common readiness to play the game by the rules of this abstraction. This fact gives rise to a contradiction: The individual expects to be treated "justly." As we have seen, there is considerable moral investment in this expectation. The expected "just" treatment, however, is possible only if the bureaucracy operates abstractly, and that means it will treat the individual "as a number." Thus the very "justice" of this treatment entails a depersonalization of each individual case. At least potentially, this constitutes a threat to the individual's self-esteem and, in the extreme case, to his subjective identity. The degree to which this threat is actually felt will depend on extrinsic factors, such as the influence of culture critics who decry the "alienating" effects of bureaucratic organization. One may safely generalize here that the threat will be felt in direct proportion to the development of individualistic and personalistic values in the consciousness of the individual. Where such values are highly developed, it is likely that the intrinsic abstraction of bureaucracy will be felt as an acute irritation at best or an intolerable oppression at worst. In such cases the "duties" of the bureaucrat collide directly with the "rights" of the client—*not*, of course, those "rights" that are bureaucratically defined and find their correlates in the "duties" of the bureaucrat, but rather those "rights" that derive from extrabureaucratic values of personal autonomy, dignity and worth. The individual whose allegiance is given to such values is almost certainly going to resent being treated "as a number." Conversely, groups in which these values have been less firmly established are likely to be less troublesome clients for bureaucracy. As we shall see later, this potential conflict between bureaucratic consciousness and the values of individual autonomy has far-reaching sociological consequences.

As in the case of technological production, bureaucratic agencies represent specific institutions. In the type of bureaucracy on which we have concentrated here, these are, of course, the institutions of the state. But in comparison with technological production, this institutional representation is more explicitly codified and sometimes protected with harsh sanctions. Thus it is not just a matter of practical utility or of custom that specific actions are performed by specific bureaucratic agencies. Rather, this is codified by legal provisions, and violations may be followed by legal penalties. The most obvious illustration of this would be a case in which an individual decides to have his passport produced in the neighborhood printing shop, or simply decides to write in his name in the passport of a deceased relative. While it is conceivable that an engineer whose job it is to deal with automobile brakes may occasionally give a hand with the engine, it is not possible to ask the sanitation department inspector to give a hand with the issuance of a passport. Thus the segmentation of the institutional order is represented more directly and fixedly in bureaucracy than it is in the sphere of technological production. This explicit segmentation may also be the source of certain discontents. For example, an individual may wish to travel outside the country while he is under a subpoena to appear in court. He may wish to discuss this problem with the official at the passport office and subsequently be irritated by the latter's stubborn refusal to assume competence in this other matter. Where there is more direct conflict with bureaucracy, this irritation may go over into an acute sense of oppression. Thus it has been a recurring theme in the student protest movement of recent years to reproach academic bureaucracy with being interested only in students' "minds" and not in their "total persons."[4] The effects of bureaucracy on identity are ambivalent. On the one hand there is an expansive effect, on the other hand a constricting one. Participation in the world of bureaucracy expands the range of the individual's identity beyond his immediate social location. For example, he becomes a man who may travel to Europe. At the same time bureaucracy limits that range. For example, he may *not* travel to Cuba. The effects on the identity of the bureaucrat himself are, of course, far more intensive, but these are outside our immediate scope.

As in the case of technological production, the effects on emotionality are primarily in terms of control—that is, bureaucracy, like technological production, imposes control upon the spontaneous expression of emotional states. But there is also a more positive aspect of this: bureaucracy *assigns* emotional states. The bracketing of personal bias, the objective assignment of cases into their appropriate boxes, the painstaking adherence to proper procedure even in situations of great stress—all of these are not just elements of cognitive style but presuppose specific emotional controls. Obviously these are more important for the bureaucrat than for his client, but to the extent that the latter participates in the rules of the bureaucratic game they will also affect his emotionality. Indeed one may raise the question whether filling out certain application forms may not require greater emotional control than handling them. Once more there are emotional frustrations ("repressions") that may arise as a result of this. Once more there develops a "second nature," this time stylized in a specific way.

The cognitive and emotional style of bureaucracy has a specific relationship to private life. Again the contrast with technological production is useful here. Private life is more easily bureaucratized than technicized precisely because human relations are more directly and concretely recognized in bureaucracy than in technology. Despite this, the individual can, perhaps paradoxically, identify more readily with his roles in the world of work ("I am an automobile worker") than with those in the world of bureaucracy ("I am an applicant"). On the other hand the individual may identify with bureaucratically assigned roles on a very abstract and anonymous level ("I am a citizen"). Furthermore in encountering bureaucracy, more "impression management" is necessary than at work.[5] Precisely because of the more arbitrary character of bureaucratic definitions of social reality, there is a greater need for deliberately manipulated self-presentation. While a worker may resort to all sorts of manipulations in order to obtain a specific job, in the end there is likely to be a hard objective testing of his performance on that job. No comparable tests are available in the world of bureaucracy. The client who knows the appropriate system of boxes may engage in elaborate operations of "impression management" to convince the bureaucrat that his case indeed fits into a particular box. It is difficult to identify with this sort of "impression management." Indeed, one of its fundamental characteristics is a fundamental disidentification between the individual and the manipulative role he is playing. Therefore in encountering bureaucracy there is always a potential emotional strain. Put differently, bureaucracy has a strong propensity to make its clients nervous.

Bureaucracy engenders very specific and peculiar modes of reciprocity. Typically, there is limited reciprocity between bureaucrat and client. The two are not mutually involved. They have different "problems." Thus the client's "problem" is to get his passport; the bureaucrat's "problem" is to get rid of the client. In other words, bureaucrats and clients are not engaged in common tasks and therefore have difficulty in reciprocally identifying with each other's roles in the process. By contrast, an engineer and an automobile worker have common problems rather frequently in their relation to the production process. There is much greater reciprocity here and at least potentially a greater chance of mutual involvement and identification. Thus it is possible in principle to speak of a morale embracing both engineers and workers in an automobile plant. Any such notion intended to embrace both bureaucrats and clients in the passport agency would be patently absurd.

A related and basically important fact is this: in his work the individual is always *actively involved*. As a client of bureaucracy he is always *passively involved*. In encountering bureaucracy, the individual does not basically do things; rather, things are done to him. Therefore the individual's encounter with bureaucracy engenders a greater sense of impotence than is typically the case with his work experience. Empirically, as seen for instance from the viewpoint of the sociological observer, this may be an illusion. Indeed, it may be the case that the individual has more opportunity to influence the bureaucracy than the management of his work situation. In other words, whatever the empirical political facts may be, the passivity that is intrinsic to the client relationship is likely to engender feelings of impotence. This sense of impotence is accentuated by two further features. First, there is the plurality of points of contact between bureaucracy and the individual's life as against the single-contact character of his relation to technological production. Most people work in only one place. Most people on the other hand encounter a variety of bureaucratic agencies. Thus the individual's relationship to technological production tends to be highly focused in terms of a particular and, to boot, highly segregated segment of his total life in society. By contrast he seems to run into bureaucracy every time he makes a move. Bureaucracy seems to encircle him quite differently from the way technological production does. This sense of being encircled can very easily go over into a bitter feeling of being besieged. Secondly, there is the fact that in encountering bureaucracy the individual typically has to deal with strangers. This, of course, is quite different from the concrete situation of the great majority of work processes. Combining these two features, one may say that encountering bureaucracy is an experience of being ongoingly surrounded by strangers.

What is the overall meaning of bureaucracy in social life?

Bureaucracy, especially in the political sphere, *locates* the individual in society more explicitly than work. It "reminds" him of his macro-social connections over and beyond his private life. Thus it is potentially more threatening or more "inspiring," as the case may be, than work. The more frequently the individual comes into contact with bureaucracy, the more frequently he is forced into structures of meaning beyond those of his private life. In the biography of many individuals this happens as their children become involved in the school system. This frequently is the source of broad political interests and engagements. This again has a moral dimension which is closely related to the way in which the political sphere as such is morally "charged."

Political bureaucracy may easily become the focus of strong interest and commitment. The moral assumptions concerning the bureaucracies of government facilitate this kind of personal investment. Unlike the world of work, bureaucracy is presumed to be there for the individual's benefit. Indeed the individual can appeal to bureaucracies (labor unions, agencies of government, courts) to do things for him *in* the world of work. We have pointed out before the bureaucratic propensity to assume that there must be an appropriate agency and an appropriate procedure for every conceivable problem in the bureaucratically assigned sector of social life. This expectation can carry over from bureaucracy to the general sphere of politics. We are then confronted with the (typically "liberal") presumption that every social problem should in principle be assigned to a specific government agency, which will presumably solve the problem through an appropriate program. This has a further important implication: while technological production may be viewed as a basic structuring force of modernity, modern man commonly copes with its impact on his own everyday life via various bureaucracies.

As we have seen, there is in bureaucracy a considerable dichotomization between bureaucrat and client as to the meaning of the institution. Therefore there is a considerable problem of legitimation. This becomes particularly evident in the comparison with technological production. While the management of such production may resort to legitimating propaganda for one purpose or another, bureaucratic agencies are much more dependent on ongoing propaganda designed to legitimate their operations and indeed their very existence. In democratic societies a good deal of this propaganda will be directed at the general public. In nondemocratic societies this propaganda will be directed toward decision-making bodies or rival groups within the bureaucracy. It goes without saying that even in democratic situations there will have to be this latter type of propaganda in addition to the appeals made to the general public.

3

Pluralization of Social Life-Worlds

To be human means to live in a world—that is, to live in a reality that is ordered and that gives sense to the business of living.[1] It is this fundamental characteristic of human existence that the term "life-world" is intended to convey. This life-world is social both in its origins and in its ongoing maintenance: the meaningful order it provides for human lives has been established collectively and is kept going by collective consent. In order to understand fully the everyday reality of any human group, it is not enough to understand the particular symbols or interaction patterns of individual situations. One must also understand the overall structure of meaning within which these particular patterns and symbols are located and from which they derive their collectively shared significance. In other words, an understanding of the social life-world is very important for the sociological analysis of concrete situations.

We believe that the above statements reflect anthropological constants. They apply to any empirically available case of human societies. Our interest here is in the specificity of modern society in this matter. We contend that one of the specific characteristics in question is the *plurality of life-worlds* in which the individual typically lives in a modern society.

Through most of human history, individuals lived in life-worlds that were more or less unified. This is not to deny that through the division of labor and other processes of institutional segmentation there have always been important differences in the life-worlds of different groups within the same society. Nevertheless, compared with modern societies, most earlier ones evinced a high degree of integration. Whatever the differences between various sectors of social life, these would "hang together" in an order of integrating meaning that included them all. This integrating order was typically religious. For the individual this meant quite simply that the *same* integrative symbols permeated the various sectors of his everyday life. Whether with his family or at work or engaged in political processes or participating in festivity and ceremonial, the individual was always in the same "world." Unless he physically left his own society, he rarely, if ever, would have the feeling that a particular social situation took him out of this common life-world. The typical situation of individuals in a modern society is very different. Different sectors of their everyday life relate them to vastly different and often severely discrepant worlds of meaning and experience. Modern life is typically segmented to a very high degree, and it is important to understand that this segmentation (or, as we prefer to call it, pluralization) is not only manifest on the level of observable social conduct but also has important manifestations on the level of consciousness.

A fundamental aspect of this pluralization is the dichotomy of private and public spheres.[2] We have already discussed this dichotomy in connection with the individual's encounters with the worlds of work and of large organizations such as those of government bureaucracy. The individual in a modern society is typically conscious of a sharp dichotomization between the world of his private life and the world of large public institutions to which he relates in a variety of roles. It is important to point out, however, that pluralization also takes place *within* these two spheres. This is obviously the case in the individual's experience in the public sphere. Thus, as we have previously mentioned, there are great differences in the world constituted by technological production and the world of bureaucracy. The individual relating to both ipso facto experiences a migration between different life-worlds.

Needless to say, these two cases do not exhaust the subject. Thus, for example, the immense complexity of the division of labor in a technological economy means that different occupations have constructed for themselves life-worlds that are not only alien but often totally incomprehensible to the outsider. At the same time the individual, regardless of his own location in the occupational system, must inevitably come into contact with a number of these segmented worlds. Let us simply imagine the typical factory worker who concerned us in an earlier chapter and accompany him as he visits, respectively, a medical clinic and a lawyer's office. But the private sphere itself is not immune to pluralization. It is indeed true that the modern individual typically tries to arrange this sphere in such a way that by contrast to his bewildering involvement with the worlds of public institutions, this private world will provide for him an order of integrative and sustaining meanings. In other words, the individual attempts to construct and maintain a "home world" which will serve as the meaningful center of his life in society. Such an enterprise is hazardous and precarious. Marriages between people of different backgrounds involve complicated negotiations between the meanings of discrepant worlds. Children habitually and disturbingly emigrate from the world of their parents. Alternate and often repulsive worlds impinge upon private life in the form of neighbors and other unwelcome intruders, and indeed it is also possible that the individual, dissatisfied for whatever reason with the organization of his private life, may himself seek out plurality in other private contacts. This quest for more satisfactory private meanings may range from extramarital affairs to experiments with exotic religious sects.

This pluralization of *both spheres* is endemic to two specifically modern experiences: the experience of urban life and the experience of modern mass communication.[3] Since its inception in ancient times the city has been a meeting place of widely different people and groups, and thus a meeting place of discrepant worlds. By its very structure the city pushes its inhabitants to be "urbane" with regard to strangers, and "sophisticated" about different approaches to reality. Modernity in any society has meant the gigantic growth of cities. This urbanization has not been only a matter of the physical growth of certain communities and the development of specifically urban institutions; urbanization is also a process on the level of consciousness, and as such it has not been limited to those communities that can properly be designated as cities.

Thus, while from census to census a larger population in the United States has been located in urban or suburban communities, an even larger proportion of the population has been urbanized in terms of consciousness. It is the city that has created the style of life (including styles of thinking, feeling and generally experiencing reality) that is now the standard for the society at large. In this sense it is possible to be "urbanized" while continuing to live in a small town or even on a farm.

This urbanization of consciousness has been brought about especially through the modern media of mass communication. The process probably began earlier with the spread of literacy as a result of modern school systems pushing outward from the city into the remotest rural hinterlands. In this sense the schoolteacher has been a carrier of "urbanity" for at least a couple of centuries. This process has been vastly accelerated, however, by technological communications media. Through mass publications, motion pictures, radio and television, the cognitive and normative definitions of reality invented in the city are rapidly diffused throughout the entire society. To be linked to these media is to be involved in the continuing urbanization of consciousness. Plurality is intrinsic to this process. The individual, wherever he may be, is bombarded with a multiplicity of information and communication. In terms of information, this process proverbially "broadens his mind." By the same token, however, it weakens the integrity and plausibility of his "home world."

In many cases, pluralization has even entered into the processes of primary socialization, that is, into those processes of childhood in which the basic formation of self and subjective world take place. Very probably this is the case with an increasing number of individuals in modern societies. The important implication of this is that such individuals not only experience the multiplication of worlds in adult life but do so from the very beginning of their social experience. Indeed it may be said that such individuals have never possessed an integrated and unchallenged "home world."[4] We shall have something to say at the end of this chapter about the implications of this for identity.

It goes without saying that pluralization of a high order is typically involved in various processes of secondary socialization in modern society, that is, socialization that occurs after the initial formation of self. Many of these processes of secondary socialization are embodied in the institutions of formal education—from nursery school to the various educational programs that socialize an individual for a particular occupation. Indeed many of these processes of secondary socialization make sense only on the basis of pluralization. Their deliberate intention is to lead the individual from one social world into another, that is, to initiate him into orders of meaning with which he was previously unacquainted and to train him in patterns of social conduct for which his previous experience did not prepare him.

We think it is important to understand the relationship of the various ideologies of "pluralism" to the plurality of social experience discussed above. We would contend that to a very large degree the former function to legitimate the latter. The coexistence of very different and often discrepant social worlds is widely legitimated in terms of such values as "democracy" and "progress." We would not deny either the sincerity of belief in these ideas or the possibility that in some cases these ideas have had objective social consequences. In general, however, it seems to us more persuasive sociologically to view the experience of plurality as prior to the various bodies of ideas that have served to legitimate it. Whatever its particular ideological coloration, every modern society must find some way to come to terms with the process of pluralization. Very probably this will entail some form of legitimation of at least a certain measure of plurality.

How does this pluralization of social life-world manifest itself in the everyday life of individuals?

To explicate this let us once more turn to a concrete situation of everyday life, a moment in which individuals engage in long-range life planning. The reader may here imagine a conversation between members of a family, particularly between husband and wife, about their common future. Such a conversation typically occurs when a particular decision has to be made—for example, a decision on whether to move geographically because of a new job opportunity. This sort of activity is, of course, located in the private sphere of an individual's social life. But because of its very nature it must touch upon larger institutional structures at almost each point.

What is the organization of knowledge implied in such long-range life planning?

A basic presupposition is that life careers are not firmly fixed but are at least relatively open. Put simply, the individual is faced with a number of alternative careers, especially in his younger years, and therefore must make decisions about these available options. It is possible for the individual to imagine himself as having different biographies. This possibility has both positive and negative consequences for the emotional economy of the individual. Positively, it may give him a feeling of freedom to shape at least certain parts of his life. Negatively, it increases the likelihood of frustration regarding specific careers. One is, after all, less likely to resign oneself to a particular situation if one believes that other situations are, in principle, possible. This frustration will be linked with feelings of regret or even guilt if the individual believes that he has missed some options or made some wrong decisions in the past. The frustration will be linked to anxiety regarding present or future decisions. Also there is likely to be a general frustration if the future seems fixed in *any* way, that is, if the individual perceives factors in his situation that inhibit or limit his sense of freedom.

There is a background of knowledge which includes a repertoire of typical life careers in the society; that is, the individual has a more or less realistic knowledge of life careers established in the society, and this knowledge provides the horizons for his own planning. In other words, in the repertoire of typical life careers there are some which are seen as being actually or potentially "filled" by oneself. These types are highly anonymous. Some of them are not encountered concretely at all in the individual's previous experience. In fantasy, usually by imaginatively reconstructing one's own past, most of these types can be "filled" by oneself. Thus a factory worker has a fairly realistic notion of the typical life career of a lawyer, even if his contacts with the social world of lawyers have been minimal or nonexistent. While the factory worker knows that he is unlikely to "fill" this particular biographical role, he can imagine without much difficulty how he might have done so if his life had taken another turn at some specific junctures. When the individual moves from fantasy to realistic reflection, he will then operate with a knowledge of the probabilities that in fact he will or will not "fill" this or that typical career.

Implicit in this scale of probabilities is a general "sociology," on whatever level of theoretical sophistication. The individual has a "map of society" within which he can locate and project himself in terms of both past biographical recollection and future projects. The individual's life is perceived as a trajectory across this "map." There is also a large body of factual knowledge, most of which is "weighted" in terms of the individual's life plans. Thus if a particular career appears to the individual as a realistically plausible project, he will have more factual knowledge about it than about a career in which he can participate only in pragmatically irrelevant fantasy. In other words, a good deal of background knowledge is related to "anticipatory socialization."[5]

Bringing together the element of planning for the future with some of the facets of consciousness discussed in the two previous chapters, we come upon a constellation that may be called *multi-relational synchronization*. This means that the individual must keep organized in his mind not only a multiplicity of social relations but also a plurality of careers that are relevant to his own life. These careers touch upon different institutional spheres and have different "timetables." In the example of a family planning a move, there are several such timetables that will almost always have to be taken into consideration. There is the general financial career of the family—for example, how will this particular move affect the husband's intention to retire at the age of sixty? There is at least one occupational career and possibly several—for example, will this move, regardless of its financial advantages, be a move up in the husband's occupational career, and if so, how will it affect the career of the wife (assuming that she too is working outside the home)? There is also a career in every marriage which expresses itself in such questions as whether a particular decision, regardless of other advantages or disadvantages, will be good or bad for the marital relationship. If there are children, a quite different timetable is involved, that of their educational careers: How are the schools and other educational opportunities in the place to which the family is considering a move? There may also be other economic timetables not directly related to the job, such as the value curve of the family's property in real estate: Would it perhaps be possible to get a better price for the house if one waits another year or two? In addition there may be various leisure-time careers of the individuals concerned: How will this move affect the husband's progress toward first position in his regional chess club, or the wife's career in a local political organization, or the children's careers in this or that sport? All these factors enter into the process of planning, which thus attains a calculuslike complexity. These careers, of course, are not necessarily separate from each other. One may influence the others, thus making the calculus even more intricate.

However vaguely this may be defined, there is the *underlying concept of a life plan,* both for the individuals and for the family unit. This life plan is the totalization of all the relevant timetables, their grand sum and their integrative meaning. In modern society, such life planning has become a value in itself. Its absence is commonly an occasion for reproach. The family unit thus operates as a life-planning workshop. A remarkably large proportion of conversations between family members (not only the adults among themselves but the adults talking with the children) relates to life planning. The life plan is subject to ongoing revision. This in turn involves an ongoing reinterpretation of the past—"I really should have done this instead of that two years ago." For most people, the principal institutional vector of life planning is the labor market and one's relation to it. In other words, the basic organizing principle for biographical projects is one's job, and other career projections typically revolve around and depend on the job.

The life plan becomes a primary source of identity. Most concrete life decisions are defined as means to an end in terms of the overall life plan. But the latter is typically open-ended and frequently defined in a very uncertain fashion. There is therefore a constant threat of frustration. If the life plan is articulated in a fairly definite way, the relevance of particular decisions to the grand project will often be doubtful and anxiety-provoking. If, on the other hand, the life plan is vague, there is likely to be anxiety of a different sort: the individual dimly knows that he *ought* to have some sort of plan, and he is made anxious and frustrated by the fact that he cannot really articulate what it is. All or most of this planning is long-range. It therefore requires a high capacity for delayed gratification. In order to further the project, the individual must wait and postpone. This brings with it a variety of additional frustrations and anxieties.

The life plan is the basic context in which knowledge of society is organized in the consciousness of the individual. Indeed, life planning is a basic organizing principle. Part of the stock of knowledge relevant to life planning is knowledge of coteries of experts who may be of assistance in this planning process. Some of them may be experts relevant to the project as a whole, for example, psychiatrists. Others are supposed to assist in major or minor portions of the project, for example, educational counselors or travel agents. Included in this body of knowledge, of course, is knowledge of the written sources of information and advice. Thus there is available to the individual a vast literature of expert advice on how to make a million on the stock market, how to improve his skills as a salesman, how to manage his wife in bed and his children in the nursery, and how to become a chess master. Since most life planning, as mentioned before, relates to a socially available repertoire of typical life careers, much of this assistance is "packageable." Different coteries of experts are prepared to supply recipes for "packaged tours" through the societal landscape. This, in turn, engenders resistances to such "packaging," particularly in the private sphere. Thus the individual is more likely to aspire to a "personalized" touch in bed than on the stock market. The resistance to "packaging" in the private sphere has led to a quest for "marginal differentiation" in life planning. Many individuals are in search of a distinctive style that will mark their career in at least the private sphere. Ironically, this quest for individual distinctiveness has also been "packaged." Thus today in the ambience of the so-called counterculture in America, there are probably several million individuals who consider themselves to be "nonconformist"—all of them using the same language, wearing the same type of clothes and exhibiting the same aesthetic symbols, and nevertheless feeling that thereby they express some highly individual originality.

What is the cognitive style of such long-range life planning?

We would again emphasize here the aspect of multi-relationality. But this must now emphatically include the self as well as others. The biography of the individual is apprehended by him as a *designed project*. This design includes identity. In other words, in long-range life planning the individual not only plans what he will do but also plans who he will be. In the case of individuals who are of great personal importance to each other, these projects overlap, both in terms of planned careers and planned identities. One individual is part of another's projects and vice versa. The family and especially the marital relationship occupy a privileged position in such project-sharing. This becomes clear as soon as one understands that identity as well as activity is part of the design. Indeed, the more "disinterested" a marriage is, the more important is this aspect: in such a case the "interest" is precisely in the realm of identity rather than in terms of this or that pragmatic goal. The "disinterested" individual marries not in order to further an occupational career or to gain social status, but in order to further the project of becoming a certain kind of person and successfully maintaining a certain "style" of life.[6]

Such life planning presupposes a specific mode of temporality. An important characteristic of this is the predominance of "in order to" motives over "because of" motives.[7] That is, the meanings of everyday life derive from future plans rather than from the explication of past events. This manner of apprehending temporality not only requires considerable effort at synchronization but also thinking in long-range time spans. This feature is related to the aspect of delayed gratification referred to previously and to the concomitant frustrations.

Large-scale projections also apply in terms of space. Individuals in a modern society move over considerable geographical territory not only in fact but also in fantasy. This physical mobility is, of course, related to projects of social mobility. American society represents a certain climax of this process. A high proportion of people in America plan their lives against the geographical backdrop of a continent. In terms of both time and space, life planning as discussed here is always a transcendence of the immediate social situation of the individual. The "map," in both its spatial and temporal dimensions, is vast. The mass of data and ideas with which the individual is bombarded by the modern communications media augments the scale of his biographical designing board. Once more this has both positive and negative implications for the individual. It may give him a sense of expansiveness and freedom. It may also mediate experiences of rootlessness and anomie.

If these are some of the characteristics of the organization of knowledge and the cognitive style implied in long-range life planning, what is the larger meaning of the latter for individual existence in modern society?

We have emphasized the centrality of life planning in the meaning the individual attributes to his own biography. At the same time it must be stressed that this meaning-giving must be related to overarching meanings of society (except perhaps in the marginal cases where an individual is projecting a highly eccentric or idiosyncratic career). As the individual plots the trajectory of his life on the societal "map," each point in his projected biography relates him to the overall web of meanings in the society. Life planning is the overarching activity *par excellence*.

All of this has very important implications for identity in modern society. By "identity" we do not mean in this context whatever entity may be thus described by a scientific psychology, but rather the actual experience of self in a particular social situation. In other words, we mean by "identity" the manner in which individuals define themselves. As such, identity is part and parcel of a specific structure of consciousness and is thus amenable to phenomenological description (regardless of this or that epistemological judgment that might be made about it by a psychologist).[8]

We have emphasized the life plan as a source for

identity. Conversely it is possible to define identity in modern society as a plan. All the peculiar aspects of modern identity can be related to this fact. Four of them should be discussed here.

Modern identity is *peculiarly open.*[9] While undoubtedly there are certain features of the individual that are more or less permanently stabilized at the conclusion of primary socialization, the modern individual is nevertheless peculiarly "unfinished" as he enters adult life. Not only does there seem to be a great objective capacity for transformations of identity in later life, but there is also a subjective awareness and even readiness for such transformations. The modern individual is not only peculiarly "conversion-prone"; he knows this and often glories in it. Biography is thus apprehended both as a migration through different social worlds and as the successive realization of a number of possible identities. The individual is not only "sophisticated" about the worlds and identities of others but also about himself. This open-ended quality of modern identity engenders psychological strains and makes the individual peculiarly vulnerable to the shifting definitions of himself by others.[10]

Modern identity is *peculiarly differentiated.*[11] Because of the plurality of social worlds in modern society, the structures of each particular world are experienced as relatively unstable and unreliable. The individual in most pre-modern societies lives in a world that is much more coherent. It therefore appears to him as firm and possibly inevitable. By contrast, the modern individual's experience of a plurality of social worlds relativizes every one of them. Consequently the institutional order undergoes a certain loss of reality. The "accent of reality"[12] consequently shifts from the objective order of institutions to the realm of subjectivity. Put differently, the individual's experience of himself becomes more real to him than his experience of the objective social world. Therefore, the individual seeks to find his "foothold" in reality in himself rather than outside himself. One consequence of this is that the individual's subjective reality (what is commonly regarded as his "psychology") becomes increasingly differentiated, complex—and "interesting" to himself. Subjectivity acquires previously unconceived "depths."

If this characteristic is coupled with the one discussed first, the crisis of modern identity becomes manifest. On the one hand, modern identity is open-ended, transitory, liable to ongoing change. On the other hand, a subjective realm of identity is the individual's main foothold in reality. Something that is constantly changing is supposed to be the *ens realissimum*. Consequently it should not be a surprise that modern man is afflicted with a *permanent identity crisis*, a condition conducive to considerable nervousness.[13]

By the same token, modern identity is *peculiarly reflective*.[14] If one exists in an integrated and intact social world, it is possible to do so with a minimum of reflection. In such cases the basic presuppositions of the social world will be taken for granted and are likely to remain so within the biographies of, at any rate, "normal" individuals. This condition of unreflected "being at home" in the social world has been classically caught in Edmund Burke's famous image of peacefully grazing English cattle—aptly used by Burke as a counter-image to the restless questioning and frenetic innovative activity of the French revolutionaries. Modern society, alas, is peculiarly inimical to such bovine tranquillity. It confronts the individual with an ever-changing kaleidoscope of social experiences and meanings. It forces him to make decisions and plans. By the same token, it forces him into reflection. Modern consciousness is therefore peculiarly aware, tense, "rationalizing." It follows that this reflectiveness pertains not only to the outside world but also to the subjectivity of the individual and especially to his identity. Not only the world but the self becomes an object of deliberate attention and sometimes anguished scrutiny.

Finally, modern identity is *peculiarly individuated.*[15] The individual, the bearer of identity as the *ens realissimum,* quite logically attains a very important place in the hierarchy of values. Individual freedom, individual autonomy and individual rights come to be taken for granted as moral imperatives of fundamental importance, and foremost among these individual rights is the right to plan and fashion one's life as freely as possible. This basic right is elaborately legitimated by a variety of modern ideologies. It is all the more important to see its rootage in fundamental structures of modern society—institutional structures as well as structures of consciousness.

The pluralization of social life-worlds has a very important effect in the area of religion.[16] Through most of empirically available human history, religion has played a vital role in providing the overarching canopy of symbols for the meaningful integration of society. The various meanings, values and beliefs operative in a society were ultimately "held together" in a comprehensive interpretation of reality that related human life to the cosmos as a whole. Indeed, from a sociological and social-psychological point of view, religion can be defined as a cognitive and normative structure that makes it possible for man to feel "at home" in the universe. This age-old function of religion is seriously threatened by pluralization. Different sectors of social life now come to be governed by widely discrepant meanings and meaning systems. Not only does it become increasingly difficult for religious traditions, and for the institutions that embody these, to integrate this plurality of social life-worlds in one overarching and comprehensive world view, but even more basically, the plausibility of religious definitions of reality is threatened from within, that is, within the subjective consciousness of the individual.

As long as religious symbols truly overarched all relevant sectors of the individual's social experience, that experience in its totality served to confirm the plausibility of the religious symbols. Put simply, almost everyone encountered by the individual in everyday life acknowledged the same overarching symbols and thus validated the credibility of these symbols. In the context of pluralization, this is no longer the case. Increasingly, as pluralization develops, the individual is forced to take cognizance of others who do not believe what he believes and whose life is dominated by different, sometimes by contradictory, meanings, values and beliefs. As a result, quite apart from other factors tending in the same direction, *pluralization has a secularizing effect*. That is, pluralization weakens the hold of religion on society and on the individual.

Institutionally, the most visible consequence of this has been the *privatization of religion*. The dichotomization of social life into public and private spheres has offered a "solution" to the religious problem of modern society. While religion has had to "evacuate" one area after another in the public sphere, it has successfully maintained itself as an expression of private meaning. Separation of church and state, autonomization of the economy as against the old religious norms, secularization of the law and of public education, loss of the church as a focus of community life—all these have been powerful trends in the modernization of society. At the same time, however, religious symbols and even (to different degrees in different countries) religious institutions have continued to have an important place in private life. People continued to utilize the old religious rites in connection with the great events of the individual life cycle, most importantly birth, marriage and death. Significantly, however, this utilization itself increasingly took pluralistic forms. Even in the private sphere, there appeared a variety of religious options. One may be baptized a Catholic, marry in a Protestant service, and—who knows?—die as a Zen Buddhist (or, for that matter, as an agnostic). The public sphere, by contrast, has come more and more to be dominated by civic creeds and ideologies with only vague religious content or sometimes no such content at all.

Social-psychologically, the same forces of pluralization have undermined the taken-for-granted status of religious meanings in individual consciousness. In the absence of consistent and general social confirmation, religious definitions of reality have lost their quality of certainty and, instead, have become matters of choice. Faith is no longer socially given, but must be individually achieved—be it by a wrenching act of decision along the lines of Pascal's "wager" or Kierkegaard's "leap"—or more trivially acquired as a "religious preference." Faith, in other words, is much harder to come by in the pluralistic situation. The individual now becomes conversion-prone, as it were. Just as his identity is liable to fundamental transformations in the course of his career through society, so is his relation to the ultimate definitions of reality.

This conception of the relationship of pluralization and secularization in no way denies that there have been other factors conducive to the latter in modern society. The rationalizing effects on consciousness described in the previous two chapters must undoubtedly be taken into account in this. While it is questionable whether modern science and modern technology are intrinsically and inevitably inimical to religion, it is clear that they have been perceived in this way by large numbers of people. At least to the extent that mystery, magic and authority have been important for human religiosity (as Dostoevsky's Grand Inquisitor maintained), the modern rationalization of consciousness has undermined the plausibility of religious definitions of reality. As a result, the secularizing effect of pluralization has gone hand in hand with other secularizing forces in modern society. The final consequence of all this can be put very simply (though the simplicity is deceptive): *modern man has suffered from a deepening condition of "homelessness."* The correlate of the migratory character of his experience of society and of self has been what might be called a metaphysical loss of "home." It goes without saying that this condition is psychologically hard to bear. It has therefore engendered its own nostalgias—nostalgias, that is, for a condition of "being at home" in society, with oneself and, ultimately, in the universe. We shall have occasion to return to this a little later in our argument.

On the Obsolescence
of the Concept of Honor

Honor occupies about the same place in contemporary usage as chastity. An individual asserting it hardly invites admiration, and one who claims to have lost it is an object of amusement rather than sympathy. Both concepts have an unambiguously outdated status in the *Weltanschauung* of modernity. Especially intellectuals, by definition in the vanguard of modernity, are about as likely to admit to honor as to be found out as chaste. At best, honor and chastity are seen as ideological leftovers in the consciousness of obsolete classes, such as military officers or ethnic grandmothers.

The obsolescence of the concept of honor is revealed very sharply in the inability of most contemporaries to understand insult, which in essence is an assault on honor. In this, at least in America, there is a close parallel between modern consciousness and modern law. Motives of honor have no standing in American law, and legal codes that still admit them, as in some countries of southern Europe, are perceived as archaic. In modern consciousness, as in American law (shaped more than any other by that prime force of modernization which is capitalism), insult in itself is not actionable, is not recognized as a real injury. The insulted party must be able to prove material damage. There are cases, indeed, where psychic harm may be the basis for a legal claim, but that too is a far cry from a notion of offense against honor. The *Weltanschauung* of everyday life closely conforms in this to the legal definitions of reality. If an individual is insulted and, as a result, is harmed in his career or his capacity to earn an income, he may not only have recourse to the courts but may count on the sympathy of his friends. His friends, and in some cases the courts, will come to his support if, say, the insult so unsettles him that he loses his self-esteem or has a nervous breakdown. If, however, neither kind of injury pertains, he will almost certainly be advised by lawyers and friends alike to just forget the whole thing. In other words, the *reality* of the offense will be denied. If the individual persists in maintaining it, he will be negatively categorized, most probably in psychiatric terms (as "neurotic," "overly sensitive," or the like), or if applicable in terms that refer to cultural lag (as "hopelessly European," perhaps, or as the victim of a "provincial mentality").

The contemporary denial of the reality of honor and of offenses against honor is so much part of a taken-for-granted world that a deliberate effort is required to even see it as a problem. The effort is worthwhile, for it can result in some, perhaps unexpected, new insights into the structure of modern consciousness.

The problem of the obsolescence of the concept of

honor can be brought into better focus by comparing it with a most timely concept—that of dignity. Taken by itself, the demise of honor might be interpreted as part of a process of moral coarsening, of a lessening of respect for persons, even of dehumanization. Indeed, this is exactly how it looked to a conservative mind at the beginning of the modern era—for example, to the fifteenth-century French poet Eustache Deschamps: "Age of decline nigh to the end,/Time of horror which does all things falsely,/Lying age, full of pride and of envy,/*Time without honour and without true judgment.*"[1] Yet it seems quite clear in retrospect that this pessimistic estimate was, to say the least, very one-sided. The age that saw the decline of honor also saw the rise of new moralities and of a new humanism, and most specifically of a historically unprecedented concern for the dignity and the rights of the individual. The same modern men who fail to understand an issue of honor are immediately disposed to concede the demands for dignity and for equal rights by almost every new group that makes them—racial or religious minorities, exploited classes, the poor, the deviant, and so on. Nor would it be just to question the genuineness of this disposition. A little thought, then, should make clear that the problem is not clarified by ethical pessimism. It is necessary to ask more fundamentally: What is honor? What is dignity? What can be learned about modern consciousness by the obsolescence of the one and the unique sway of the other?

Honor is commonly understood as an aristocratic concept, or at least associated with a hierarchical order of society. It is certainly true that Western notions of honor have been strongly influenced by the medieval codes of chivalry and that these were rooted in the social structures of feudalism. It is also true that concepts of honor have survived into the modern era best in groups retaining a hierarchical view of society, such as the nobility, the military, and traditional professions like law and medicine. In such groups honor is a direct expression of status, a source of solidarity among social equals and a demarcation line against social inferiors. Honor, indeed, also dictates certain standards of behavior in dealing with inferiors, but the full code of honor only applies among those who share the same status in the hierarchy. In a hierarchically ordered society the etiquette of everyday life consists of ongoing transactions of honor, and different groups relate differently to this process according to the principle of "To each his due." It would be a mistake, however, to understand honor *only* in terms of hierarchy and its delineations. To take the most obvious example, the honor of women in many traditional societies, while usually differentiated along class lines, may pertain in principle to women of *all* classes.

J. K. Campbell, in his study of contemporary rural culture in Greece,[2] makes this very clear. While the obligations of honor (*timi*) differ as between different categories of individuals, notably between men and women, everyone within the community exists within the same all-embracing system of honor. Those who have high status in the community have particular obligations of honor, but even the lowly are differentiated in terms of honor and dishonor. Men should exhibit manliness and women shame, but the failure of either implies dishonor for the individual, the family and, in some cases, the entire community. For all, the qualities enjoined by honor provide the link, not only between self and community, but between self and the idealized norms of the community: "Honour considered as the possession by men and women of these qualities is the attempt to relate existence to certain archetypal patterns of behaviour."³ Conversely, dishonor is a fall from grace in the most comprehensive sense —loss of face in the community, but also loss of self and separation from the basic norms that govern human life.

It is valid to view such a culture as essentially premodern, just as it is plausible to predict its disintegration under the impact of modernization. Historically, there are several stages in the latter process. The decline of medieval codes of honor did not lead directly to the contemporary situation in which honor is an all but meaningless concept. There took place first the *embourgeoisement* of honor, which has been defined by Norbert Elias as the process of "civilization," both a broadening and a mellowing process.⁴ The contents had changed, but there was still a conception of honor in the age of the triumphant bourgeoisie. Yet it was with the rise of the bourgeoisie, particularly in the consciousness of its critical intellectuals, that not only the honor of the *ancien régime* and its hierarchical prototypes was debunked, but that an understanding of man and society emerged that would eventually liquidate *any* conception of honor.

Thus Cervantes' *Quixote* is the tragi-comedy of a particular obsolescence, that of the knight-errant in an age in which chivalry has become an empty rhetoric. The greatness of the *Quixote*, however, transcends this particular time-bound debunking job. It unmasks not only the "madness" of chivalry but, by extension, the folly of *any* identification of self with "archetypal patterns of behaviour." Put differently, Don Quixote's "enchanters" (whose task, paradoxically, is precisely what Max Weber had in mind as "*dis*enchantment") cannot be stopped so easily once they have started their terrible task. As Don Quixote tells Sancho in one of his innumerable homilies: "Is it

possible that in the time you have been with me you have
not yet found out that all the adventures of a knight-
errant appear to be illusion, follies, and dreams, and turn
out to be the reverse? Not because things are really so,
but because in our midst there is a host of enchanters,
forever changing, disguising and transforming our affairs
as they please, according to whether they wish to favor or
destroy us. So, what you call a barber's basin is to me
Mambrino's helmet, and to another person it will appear
to be something else."[5] These "enchanters," alas, have not
stopped with chivalry. Every human adventure, in which
the self and its actions have been identified and endowed
with the honor of collective prototypes has, finally, been
debunked as "illusion, follies, and dreams." Modern man
is Don Quixote on his deathbed, denuded of the multi-
colored banners that previously enveloped the self and
revealed to be *nothing but a man:* "I was mad, but I am
now in my senses; I was once Don Quixote of La Mancha,
but I am now, as I said before, Alonso Quixano the
Good."[6] The same self, deprived or, if one prefers, freed
from the mystifications of honor is hailed in Falstaff's
"catechism": "Honour is a mere scutcheon."[7] It is modern
consciousness that unmasks it as such, that "enchants" or
"disenchants" it (depending on one's point of view) until
it is shown as nothing but a painted artifact. Behind the
"mere scutcheon" is the face of modern man—man bereft
of the consolation of prototypes, *man alone.*

It is important to understand that it is precisely this
solitary self that modern consciousness has perceived as
the bearer of human dignity and of inalienable human
rights. The modern discovery of dignity took place precisely amid the wreckage of debunked conceptions of
honor. Now, it would be a mistake to ascribe to modern
consciousness alone the discovery of a fundamental dig-

nity underlying all possible social disguises. The same discovery can be found in the Hebrew Bible, as in the confrontation between Nathan and David ("Thou art the man"); in Sophocles, in the confrontation between Antigone and Creon; and, in a different form, in Mencius' parable of a criminal stopping a child from falling into a well. The understanding that there is a humanity behind or beneath the roles and the norms imposed by society, and that this humanity has profound dignity, is not a modern prerogative. What is peculiarly modern is the manner in which the reality of this intrinsic humanity is related to the realities of society.

Dignity, as against honor, always relates to the intrinsic humanity divested of all socially imposed roles or norms. It pertains to the self as such, to the individual regardless of his position in society. This becomes very clear in the classic formulations of human rights, from the Preamble to the Declaration of Independence to the Universal Declaration of Human Rights of the United Nations. These rights always pertain to the individual "irrespective of race, color or creed"—or, indeed, of sex, age, physical condition or any conceivable social status. There is an implicit sociology and an implicit anthropology here. The implicit sociology views all biological and historical differentiations among men as either downright unreal or essentially irrelevant. The implicit anthropology locates the real self over and beyond all these differentiations.

It should now be possible to see these two concepts somewhat more clearly. Both honor and dignity are concepts that bridge self and society. While either pertains to the individual in a very intimate way, it is in relations with others that both honor and dignity are attained, exchanged, preserved or threatened. Both require a deliberate effort of the will for their maintenance—one must *strive* for them, often against the malevolent opposition of others—thus honor and dignity become goals of moral enterprise. Their loss, always a possibility, has far-reaching consequences for the self. Finally, both honor and dignity have an infectious quality that extends beyond the moral person of the individual possessing them. The infection involves his body ("a dignified gait"), his material ambience (from clothing to the furnishings of his house) and other individuals closely associated with him ("He brought honor on his whole family"). What, then, is the difference between these two concepts of the social self? Or, substituting a more current term to avoid the metaphysical associations of "self," how do these two conceptions of identity differ?

The concept of honor implies that identity is essentially, or at least importantly, linked to institutional roles. The modern concept of dignity, by contrast, implies that identity is essentially independent of institutional roles. To return to Falstaff's image, in a world of honor the individual *is* the social symbols emblazoned on his escutcheon. The true self of the knight is revealed as he rides out to do battle in the full regalia of his role; by comparison, the naked man in bed with a woman represents a lesser reality of the self. In a world of dignity, in the modern sense, the social symbolism governing the interaction of men is a disguise. The escutcheons *hide* the true self. It is precisely the naked man, and even more specifically the naked man expressing his sexuality, who represents himself more truthfully. Consequently, the understanding of self-discovery and self-mystification is reversed as between these two worlds. In a world of honor, the individual discovers his true identity in his roles, and to turn away from the

roles is to turn away from himself—in "false consciousness," one is tempted to add. In a world of dignity, the
individual can only discover his true identity by emanci-
pating himself from his socially imposed roles—the latter
are only masks, entangling him in illusion, "alienation"
and "bad faith." It follows that the two worlds have a different relation to history. It is through the performance
of institutional roles that the individual participates in
history, not only the history of the particular institution
but that of his society as a whole. It is precisely for this
reason that modern consciousness, in its conception of
the self, tends toward a curious ahistoricity. In a world of
honor, identity is firmly linked to the past through the
reiterated performance of prototypical acts. In a world of
dignity, history is the succession of mystifications from
which the individual must free himself to attain "authenticity."

It is important not to lose sight here of continuities in
the constitution of man—of "anthropological constants,"
if one prefers. Modern man is not a total innovation or a
mutation of the species. Thus he shares with any version
of archaic man known to us both his intrinsic sociality
and the reciprocal process with society through which his
various identities are formed, maintained and changed.
All the same, within the parameters set by his fundamental constitution, man has considerable leeway in constructing, dismantling and reassembling the worlds in
which he lives. Inasmuch as identity is always part of a
comprehensive world, and a humanly *constructed* world
at that, there are far-reaching differences in the ways in
which identity is conceived and, consequently, experienced. Definitions of identity vary with overall definitions
of reality. Each such definition, however, has reality-gen-

erating power: Men not only define themselves, but they actualize these definitions in real experience—*they live them.*

No monocausal theory is likely to do justice to the transformation that has taken place. Very probably most of the factors commonly cited have in fact played a part in the process—technology and industrialization, bureaucracy, urbanization and population growth, the vast increase in communication between every conceivable human group, social mobility, the pluralization of social worlds and the profound metamorphosis in the social contexts in which children are reared. Be this as it may, the resultant situation has been aptly characterized by Arnold Gehlen with the terms "de-institutionalization" and "subjectivization." The former term refers to a global weakening in the holding power of institutions over the individual. The institutional fabric, whose basic function has always been to provide meaning and stability for the individual, has become incohesive, fragmented and thus progressively deprived of plausibility. The institutions then confront the individual as fluid and unreliable, in the extreme case as unreal. Inevitably, the individual is thrown back upon himself, on his own subjectivity, from which he must dredge up the meaning and the stability that he requires to exist. Precisely because of man's intrinsic sociality, this is a very unsatisfactory condition. Stable identities (and this also means identities that will be subjectively plausible) can only emerge in reciprocity with stable social contexts (and this means contexts that are structured by stable institutions). Therefore, there is a deep uncertainty about contemporary identity. Put differently, there is a built-in identity crisis in the contemporary situation.

It is in this connection that one begins to understand

the implicit sociology and the implicit anthropology mentioned above. Both are rooted in actual experience of the modern world. The literary, philosophical and even social-scientific formulations are ex post facto attempts to come to terms with this experience. Gehlen has shown this convincingly for the rise of the modern novel as the literary form most fully reflecting the new subjectivism. But the conceptualizations of man and society of, for instance, Marxism and existentialism are equally rooted in this experience. So is the perspective of modern social science, especially of sociology. Marx's "alienation" and "false consciousness," Heidegger's "authenticity" and Sartre's "bad faith," and such current sociological notions as David Riesman's "other-direction" or Erving Goffman's "impression management" could only arise and claim credibility in a situation in which the identity-defining power of institutions has been greatly weakened.

The obsolescence of the concept of honor may now be seen in a much more comprehensive perspective. The social location of honor lies in a world of relatively intact, stable institutions, a world in which individuals can with subjective certainty attach their identities to the institutional roles that society assigns to them. The disintegration of this world as a result of the forces of modernity has not only made honor an increasingly meaningless notion, but has served as the occasion for a redefinition of identity and its intrinsic dignity apart from and often *against* the institutional roles through which the individual expresses himself in society. The reciprocity between individual and society, between subjective identity and objective identification through roles, now comes to be experienced as a sort of struggle. Institutions cease to be the "home" of the self; instead they become oppressive realities that distort and estrange the self. Roles no longer actualize the self, but serve as a "veil of *maya*" hiding the self not only from others but from the individual's own consciousness. Only in the interstitial areas left vacant, as it were, by the institutions (such as the so-called private sphere of social life) can the individual hope to discover or define himself. Identity ceases to be an objectively and subjectively given fact, and instead becomes the goal of an often devious and difficult quest. Modern man, almost inevitably it seems, is ever in search of himself. If this is understood, it will also be clear why both the sense of "alienation" and the concomitant identity crisis are most vehement among the young today. Indeed, "youth" itself, which is a matter of social definition rather than biological fact, will be seen as an interstitial area vacated or "left over" by the large institutional structures of modern society. For this reason it is, simultaneously, the locale of the most acute experiences of self-estrangement and of the most intensive quest for reliable identities.

A lot will depend, naturally, on one's basic assumptions about man whether one will bemoan or welcome these transformations. What to one will appear as a profound loss will be seen by another as the prelude to liberation. Among intellectuals today, of course, it is the latter viewpoint that prevails and that forms the implicit anthropological foundation for the generally "left" mood of the time. The threat of chaos, both social and psychic, which ever lurks behind the disintegration of institutions, will then be seen as a necessary stage that must precede the great "leap into freedom" that is to come. It is also possible, in a conservative perspective, to view the same process as precisely the root pathology of the modern era, as a disastrous loss of the very structures that enable men to be free and to be themselves. Such pessimism is expressed forcefully, if somewhat petulantly, in Gehlen's latest book, a conservative manifesto in which modernity appears as an all-engulfing pestilence.[8]

We would contend here that both perspectives—the liberation myth of the "left" and the nostalgia of the "right" for an intact world—fail to do justice to the anthropological and indeed the ethical dimensions of the problem. It seems clear to us that the unrestrained enthusiasm for total liberation of the self from the "repression" of institutions fails to take account of certain fundamental requirements of man, notably those of *order*—that institutional order of society without which both collectivities and individuals must descend into dehumanizing chaos. In other words, the demise of honor has been a very costly price to pay for whatever liberations modern man may have achieved. On the other hand, the unqualified denunciation of the contemporary constellation of institutions and identities fails to perceive the vast moral achievements made possible by just this constellation—the discovery of the autonomous individual, with a dignity deriving from his very being, over and above all and any social identifications. Anyone denouncing the modern world *tout court* should pause and question whether he wishes to include in that denunciation the specifically modern discoveries of human dignity and human rights. The conviction that even the weakest members of society have an inherent right to protection and dignity; the proscription of slavery in all its forms, of racial and ethnic oppression; the staggering discovery of the dignity and rights of the child; the new sensitivity to cruelty, from the abhorrence of torture to the codification of the crime of genocide—a sensitivity that has become politically significant in the outrage against the cruelties of the war in Vietnam; the new recognition of individual responsibility for all actions, even those assigned to the individual with specific institutional roles, a recognition that attained the force of law at Nuremberg—all these, and others, are moral achievements that would be unthinkable without the peculiar constellations of the modern world. To reject them is unthinkable ethically. By the same token, it is not possible to simply trace them to a false anthropology.

The task before us, rather, is to understand the empirical processes that have made modern man lose sight of honor at the expense of dignity—and then to think through both the anthropological and the ethical implications of this. Obviously these remarks can do no more than point up some dimensions of the problem. It may be allowed, though, to speculate that a rediscovery of honor in the future development of modern society is both empirically plausible and morally desirable. Needless to say, this will hardly take the form of a regressive restoration of traditional codes. But the contemporary mood of anti-institutionalism is unlikely to last, as Anton Zijderveld implies.[9] Man's fundamental constitution is such that, just about inevitably, he will once more construct institutions to provide an ordered reality for himself. A return to institutions will ipso facto be a return to honor. It will then be possible again for individuals to identify themselves with the escutcheons of their institutional roles, experienced now not as self-estranging tyrannies but as freely chosen vehicles of self-realization. The ethical question, of course, is what these institutions will be like. Specifically, the ethical test of any future institutions, and of the codes of honor they will entail, will be whether they succeed in embodying and in stabilizing the discoveries of human dignity that are the principal achievements of modern man.

Modern Consciousness: Packages and Carriers

In the foregoing chapters we have tried to explicate the relationships between certain institutional processes which are commonly taken to be typically modern and certain constellations of consciousness. As far as possible we have tried to focus on such of the latter as appear to us to be endemic, perhaps even necessary, to these institutional processes—that is, we have tried to clarify certain *intrinsic relations* between modern institutions and modern consciousness, or, to put it differently, we have tried to bring out clusters of consciousness that are *intrinsic properties* of certain modern institutions. Yet even in the foregoing discussion it has become clear that the empirical relationships are of very great complexity, both on the institutional level and on the level of consciousness. In addition to the constellations of consciousness that are intrinsic to modern institutions, there are many that can only be called *extrinsic* and that are empirically linked to these institutions as a result of a great variety of historical processes. What manifests itself empirically as modern consciousness is a highly complex combination of these "necessary" and "accidental" elements.

Any attempt to delineate the character of modernity solely on the basis of a phenomenological description of intrinsic constellations of consciousness would therefore be methodologically inadmissible. Indeed it would be a kind of historical determinism ("idealistic" or "materialistic," depending on which of the two levels of analysis one would assign causal primacy to) which could only result in a gross distortion of empirical reality. So in order to do justice to our topic, we must pass from the level of phenomenological description to that of institutional analysis, or rather we must seek to build bridges between these two. This presents us with vastly difficult and intellectually risky problems.

To assist us in this task let us introduce two concepts at this point. The first is the concept of *package*.[1] By this we mean an empirically available linkage of institutional processes and clusters of consciousness, which may be composed of intrinsically or extrinsically linked elements. The second is the concept of *carrier*.[2] By this we mean an institutional process or a group that has produced or transmitted a particular element of consciousness. Again, this relationship may be either intrinsic or extrinsic, "necessary" or "accidental."

For example, we have argued that there is an intrinsic linkage between technological production and the element of cognitive style we have called componentiality. We are confronted here with a package of intrinsically linked elements. In other words, once technological production is given, it is very hard to "think away" the element of componentiality. In America, however, the package carried by the institutions of technological production also contains elements derived from the economic ethos of capitalism—for example, the motives of individual competition and profit-making geared to the accumulation of private property. In theory, these latter elements can be "thought away" from the processes of technological production, and they have been substantially reduced in some empirically available socialist economies. They are therefore extrinsic properties of this particular package.

As another example, we have argued that there is an intrinsic linkage between bureaucracy and what we have called the taxonomic style. In America the package carried by bureaucracy also contains values derived from the ethos of political democracy, such as the accountability of bureaucratic agencies to a democratically constituted political structure, or the obligation of bureaucrats to safeguard the democratically legitimated civil liberties of the individual. Once again, these values may be viewed as extrinsic to bureaucracy as such and linked to it in a package produced by a variety of historical "accidents."

Similar considerations apply to the carriers themselves. For instance, bureaucracy as an institution and bureaucrats as a group obviously serve as carriers of the constellations of consciousness in question. We may assume that they do so by virtue of their intrinsic character. On the other hand it is quite possible that the same constellations of consciousness are also carried by other institutions or groups. The educational system or the military might be cited as cases in point. In these cases it is quite possible to "think away" the clusters of consciousness in question, and indeed we have empirically available to us cases of education and of the military without these bureaucratic characteristics. In other words, we are confronted here with institutions and groups that have come to be extrinsically linked to these particular packages. This, of course, makes it all the more necessary to explore the historical processes by which the linkage came about.

At this stage of our argument it is necessary to say something about the *variant institutional vectors* that are relevant to the structures of consciousness previously described. It would be very satisfying if at this point we could present a comprehensive theory of modern institutions. Unfortunately, we are not intrepid enough to do this. On the other hand, we are not faced with an insuperable task either. There is a large body of sociological theory and findings to which we can have recourse.

The peculiarity of modern institutions has, after all, been a central theme of sociological thought since its beginnings in the nineteenth century. It has followed two major traditions: that of Marxism and that of classical (in Marxist terms "bourgeois") sociology. Marxism explains the peculiarity of modern institutions almost entirely in terms of the peculiarity of modern capitalism. It takes capitalism's "property relations" as *the* determining variable for contemporary society. All other features of society then become dependent variables, although, of course, different Marxist schools differ as to the precise character of the dependency. Marxism traces the roots of modern consciousness in all its major constellations to modern capitalism (a procedure which, because of the philosophical-anthropological presuppositions of Marxism, eventuates in a diagnosis of "false consciousness.")

We have already indicated that we consider this a very one-sided and therefore distorted perspective on the level of consciousness. We consider it equally so on the level of institutional analysis. To be sure, capitalism has been an exceedingly important force in the creation of modernity, but it has not been the only force. We place ourselves in the other tradition, that of classical sociology, in our understanding of modern society's institutional dynamics. Indeed, it is remarkable how much convergence, despite all differences, there has been in the theoretical explications of this tradition. Of central relevance to our present concern is Emile Durkheim's view of the transition from mechanical to organic solidarity, Ferdinand Toennies' conceptualization of *Gemeinschaft* and *Gesellschaft*, Max Weber's theory of rationalization, Talcott Parsons' view of the shifts in pattern variables, and Marion Levy's view of the shift in the structural features of society in the course of modernization.[3] We ourselves find the Weberian approach to these matters the most satisfactory.[4]

Basic to the Weberian approach is the conception of causal reciprocity between institutional processes and processes on the level of consciousness. This reciprocity is what Weber called "elective affinity." His basic theoretical intention was to give due credit to the effect of institutional processes on human ideas, values and beliefs, while at the same time avoiding the one-sided determinism that he (rightly or wrongly) associated with Marx. Thus, according to Weber, certain historical transfigurations of consciousness are to be seen as preconditions for modern society. In Weber's own work, of course, major emphasis was placed upon the emergence of the "Protestant ethic," that constellation of values and attitudes that he regarded as crucial for the emergence of modern capitalism.[5] However, the institutions resulting from these transformations of consciousness (including those of modern capitalism) are not to be understood as continuing to be dependent on the constellations of consciousness that originally gave birth to them. Weber was fully aware that the Protestant ethic could in no way explain the motives and actions of people in the capitalist economy of his day. Rather, institutions, once established, develop a dynamic of their own and, in turn, have effects of their own on the level of consciousness. These effects are capable of autonomous development. Thus both institutional processes and processes on the level of consciousness are capable of developing autonomously, sometimes for considerable periods of time, while on other occasions, in terms of the concept of elective affinity, they may be viewed as "seeking each other out." To return to the concepts we introduced a short time ago, institutional carriers "discard" their erstwhile "baggage" of packages of consciousness. Conversely, the latter can "go off on their own" and leave behind the institutional contexts to which they were originally linked.

Following Weber, we see the decisive institutional vectors for modernity in the economic and political areas. Historically, the modernizing institutions *par excellence* have been *modern industrial capitalism* and the *modern bureaucratic state*. To a large extent they still are, though a number of important developments have now to be taken into account. The most important of these is that since the industrial revolution technological production has acquired an autonomous dynamic (and rationalizing force) of its own, which is no longer necessarily linked to the particular economic arrangements of capitalism. (We touched on this in our discussion of the relationship of technological production to modern consciousness.) It is therefore not possible to relate the constellations of consciousness discussed merely to those technological economies whose form of organization is capitalistic; a socialistic organization of the economy, whatever other differences it may bring about, will confront very similar if not the same configurations that we discussed.

In terms of modern consciousness in the contemporary world we must differentiate between *primary* and *secondary carriers*. Primary carriers are, first, technological production (whatever its specific economic and social organization), and second, the bureaucratically organized state (whatever its other political or ideological features). We consider these two not only the primary carriers of modern consciousness but, by the same logic, the primary agents of modernization. It is important to stress that while empirically these two institutional forces have often operated in conjunction, they may also operate separately. Indeed, in line with our previous discussion of the differences in the structures of consciousness as between these two carriers, we would expect that considerable differences will be found on the level of consciousness, depending on whether the one or the other carrier is the dominant force in a particular situation.

Secondary carriers include a variety of social and cultural processes, most of them *historically* grounded in the primary carriers but now capable of autonomous efficacy. Among these we would particularly stress the following: urbanization; a "mobilized" stratification system; the "private sphere" as a key context of individual life; the distinctive institutions of scientific and technological innovation; mass education and, as an extension of it, the mass media of communication.

We have already touched on most of these in our discussion of the pluralization of social life-worlds, but some further comment may be in order here. Urbanization, both in the literal sense of the growth of cities and also in the sense of the diffusion of urban life styles, may certainly be considered an independent carrier of modern consciousness today. While most urban development in the modern world has been closely tied to developments in the economy, in terms of both trade and manufacturing, urbanism today is a phenomenon that must be understood in its own terms regardless of a particular economic context. Closely related to urbanization in this broad sense is the great increase in social mobility as between different strata in modern society. While modernization generally means a real increase in the ability of people to move from one stratum to another, in many cases (certainly in America) the expectations of social mobility have been much greater than its realistic chances for most individuals. These very expectations, however, are of great importance for what happens on the level of consciousness.[6] Whatever may be an individual's realistic probabilities of greatly improving his position within the stratification of his society, his imagination, by virtue of "anticipatory socialization," will range far and wide in social sectors that are very distant from his biographical starting position in society. This "mobilization" (in the sense of making more mobile) of the imagination may be seen as separate from the economic structure which generally determines the extent to which mobility aspirations can be satisfied.[7]

We have already discussed at some length the great importance of the "private sphere" and the dichotomization of both social life and consciousness that it has engendered. We have not previously discussed and cannot discuss at any length those institutions of the modern world that are designed to guarantee continuing advances in science and technology. We are thinking here of the vast network of what Fritz Machlup has called the "knowledge industry."[8] In this network of institutions devoted to cerebration, research and the diffusion of scientific and technological innovations, ongoing modifications of consciousness are produced by an elite whose social mission is explicitly defined in those terms. While clearly only a small minority of the population belongs to this elite, its actions directly affect not only the practical lives but also the consciousness of the rest of the population. As we have seen in our discussion of technological production, despite the fact that, for example, production workers do not directly share in the lore of modern science and technology, this lore serves as an important horizon to their consciousness and directly impinges upon it in a number of places.

The importance of mass education and the mass media for modern consciousness hardly needs much elaboration in the present context. The important thing here is to stress once more that these secondary carriers can operate as factors quite independent of any other. For example, it is possible for a modern communications medium to "reach into" a situation (as in many Third World societies) that has not been touched by any other modernizing force, either primary or secondary. Similarly mass education, while it certainly cannot be considered an important factor in the creation of the modern world historically, is today a modernizing force of very great importance indeed.[9]

In the absence of a comprehensive and definitive theory of modern institutions, any statements about institutional vectors of modern consciousness will have to be hypothetical. We would therefore like to emphasize very strongly that the following discussion is strictly hypothetical, by which we mean not only that we do not claim to be sure about what follows, but also that these matters are amenable to empirical investigation. With these reservations we suggest that the following are variant institutional vectors of significance for modern consciousness.

(1) *the degree of development of the primary carriers.* A significant variant for modern consciousness is whether the primary carriers are more or less "advanced." In the case of the first primary carrier this means, of course, the degree of economic and technological "development"; in the case of the second, the degree of "development" in terms of modern political institutions. In each case the most meaningful way to look at these matters is by conceiving them as continua.[10]

(2) *the cultural location of the primary carriers.* A significant variant is whether the primary carriers are culturally indigenous or culturally imported. Needless to say this is a particularly important variant to look into when comparing "development" in the so-called Third World today with the history of Western industrial societies.

(3) *access to the economic benefits of modernity.* Modern technological production has enormously increased the affluence of certain societies. However, both within these societies and in the relationships of other societies to them, there continue to be enormous differences in terms of access to these economic benefits. Some groups directly participate in these benefits, while others relate to the processes of modern production in much more marginal ways, or indeed by way of being exploited by them. Put simply, some groups are rich by virtue of their relationship to modern technological production, while others have remained poor or have even been impoverished as a result of this relationship. In other words, the analytic import of this particular variant is the question as to whose ox is being gored.

(4) *the social organization of the economy.* While technological production is viewed by us as a primary social force, this force can be organized in different ways. The most important differentiation in terms of the contemporary world is that between capitalist and socialist forms. As we have argued before, this variant does not, in our opinion, affect the intrinsic packages carried by technological production. However, there are important extrinsic modifications of both institutions and consciousness that must be taken into account.

(5) *the degree of bureaucratic autonomy.* Bureaucratic organization, as we have tried to show, engenders a dynamic of its own on the level of social action and on the level of consciousness. Bureaucracy, however, operates in quite different social and political contexts. The most important variant is whether bureaucratic organization operates with or without external restraints upon it, or, more precisely, the variant to be taken into account concerns the *degree* of such external restraints.[11] Put simply, some bureaucracies have nothing to worry about except themselves; other bureaucracies have to put up with such intrinsically irrelevant inconveniences as legal restraints or public opinion.

To repeat, while we do not claim that this list is either axiomatic or complete, we hypothesize that the aforementioned variants cover the most important institutional vectors for modern consciousness. We will return to them in greater detail in the following chapter.

Our basic question in these considerations has been: Which packages can be taken apart and which cannot? The foregoing considerations relate to this basic question by way of two master hypotheses:

(1) *There are more intrinsic linkages between institutional processes and clusters of consciousness in the*

case of the primary carriers than in the case of other carriers. Put differently, the packages relating to the primary carriers are more firmly "tied together" and therefore more difficult to take apart. To the extent that this hypothesis holds, we can propose a rule of thumb for any projects that involve a restructuring of consciousness, to wit, such projects have a likelihood of succeeding that is inversely proportional to their closeness to the primary carriers.

(2) *As between the primary carriers themselves, there are more intrinsic linkages between institutional processes and clusters of consciousness in the case of technological production than in the case of bureaucracy.* In other words, economic forces are more "compelling" than political forces on the level of consciousness. We have already explained why we believe this in our discussion of the relation of these two carriers to modern consciousness.

We cannot presume to validate or invalidate these hypotheses in the context of this book. Such an undertaking would have to be enormous in scope, and even then we have some doubts whether the available data would be sufficient to allow anyone to make definitive statements. How ver, having explicated the logic underlying our hypotheses, we can now continue to draw out the implications of this particular way of asking questions about modernity: we turn from institutional vectors to the level of consciousness and the *symbolic universe* of modernity. What we mean by this term is essentially simple: Social life is permeated by a network of cognitive and normative definitions of reality. These have differential locations within consciousness and relate in different ways to different sectors of the institutional order. However, for a society to serve as a common context for individual life and action there must be an all-embracing

frame of reference for at least most of these definitions of
reality, and this frame of reference must be shared by
at least most members of the society. The symbolic universe of a society is a body of tradition that integrates a
large number of definitions of reality and presents the
institutional order to the individual as a symbolic totality.[12] In other words, our question now concerns what has
often been called the *Weltanschauung* of modernity.

From everything that has been said before, it should
be clear that this cannot be considered a firmly crystallized or logically coherent body of reality definitions. It
should also be clear that whatever the symbolic universe
of modernity may be in its specific details, it is unlikely
to be causally traceable to a few invariant institutional
factors (let alone one such factor). We may assume that
the symbolic universe of modern societies will be a loosely
assembled and far from stable constellation of reality
definitions. Often it will be grossly lacking in logical
consistency. Always it will be related to a number of institutional carriers that are themselves constantly changing. The relation of this modern world view to institutional carriers will evince once more an empirical
coexistence of intrinsic and extrinsic elements of consciousness, that is, of "necessity" and "accident."

The best word to describe what we have in mind
here would be the French word *briccolage*,[13] which is
used for the activity by which a child puts together and
takes apart the pieces of a construction set. It is very
salutary to think of modern *Weltanschauung* in such
terms, especially in view of the continuing tendency of
a number of culture critics (and culture prophets!) to
tell us with apodictic certainty just what "modern man"
is and just what is allegedly inevitable about his view of
the world. The various theories about "modern man" and

his *Weltanschauung* which have been concocted for at least the last hundred years are themselves an interesting topic for the sociology of knowledge, a topic which, unfortunately, we cannot pursue here. We suggest an attitude of sharp skepticism toward most of these theories. Their overall tendency has been to simplify and often to obfuscate the situation. The alternative to this type of simplification, however, is *not* some sort of hushed awe before the allegedly irreducible diversity of the human spirit (let alone before some alleged mystery, redemptive or malign, of modern man). These phenomena are quite amenable to theoretical clarification as well as empirical investigation. Instead of adding to the various pronunciamentos concerning modern man and his putative consciousness, we would like to suggest a process of careful and necessarily tentative analysis.

If we hypothesize that technological production and bureaucracy constitute primary carriers of modern consciousness, and if we understand that the packages pertaining to these carriers combine in a variety of ways with elements of consciousness deriving from elsewhere, then the following question becomes relevant: *Which specific themes of the symbolic universe of modernity are intrinsically derived from the primary carriers?* We can put the same question differently: What themes for an overarching world view are intrinsically contributed by technological production and bureaucracy?

Let us consider technological production first. Technological work has an ambivalent place in the symbolic universe of modernity. On the one hand, it has directly shaped the latter. On the other hand, it has also engendered strong reactions against it. We find a recurring ambivalence of componentiality on the one hand and of a renewed quest for "wholeness" on the other. We should also note that aspects of the symbolic universe of modernity (we may refer here once more to Weber's discussion of the Protestant ethic) antedate modern technological production and indeed were a precondition for it. At the same time, these aspects are now greatly reinforced by the situation brought about by modern industrial production.

Generally speaking, the "world of work" occupies a dominant position in the social life of any society.[14] This has probably always been the case, but it has been the case more than ever because of the tremendous impact of modern technological production upon every facet of social life. The themes derived from this form of production dominate the reality of social life. Indeed other forms of social experience are defined as enclaves within or refuges from the "world of work." The individual's "private sphere" is, as it were, "surrounded" by the large economic or bureaucratic institutions to which he relates through his job. In order really to remove himself from the dominance of the "world of work" he must either literally or figuratively "go on vacation." Such a "vacation" always involves a deliberate and often very difficult effort to shake off precisely that reality that is foremost in the individual's work life. Whatever the resistances or reactions against the packages derived from this primary carrier, work life is of paramount importance to most people in a contemporary society.

Not all the themes previously discussed in connection with technological production are "transferable" to the symbolic universe as a whole. Some, particularly the following, are.

First: *Rationality*. This, as Weber saw most clearly, is a key theme. This does not mean the reflective rationality engaged in by a scientist or philosopher, but rather immediately available functional rationality, rationality as it is thematizable in the everyday life of the individual.

Second: *Componentiality*. As we have seen, reality is apprehended as being constituted by clearly separable components which relate to each other in structures of causality, time and space. This theme is introduced into experiences of both others and self, and becomes an overarching theme for the symbolic universe as such.

Third: *Multi-relationality*. This, as we have seen, relates to the enormous variety of relations—with other people, with material objects and with abstract entities—that the individual must hold present in his consciousness when relating to the processes of technological production. Ongoing "practice" in multi-relationality constitutes a field of consciousness in terms of such manifold relations. This becomes a constituent element of the symbolic universe, that is, it is "transferred" from the realm of technological production to other spheres of social life and consciousness.

Fourth: *"Makeability."* What is involved here is a problem-solving approach to reality which is apprehended as "makeable." Life (including social experience and identity) is seen as an ongoing problem-solving enterprise.

Fifth: *Plurality*. As Alfred Schutz has shown, "multiple realities" are a constant and probably necessary feature of human consciousness.[15] The capacity to move from what Schutz calls the "paramount reality" of everyday life to other spheres of meaning may be assumed to be anthropologically given. What happens under modern conditions, however, is that this given capacity is vastly intensified. Plurality becomes a basic theme of life. With this pluralization, the creation of any overarching symbolic universe becomes increasingly more difficult. Different realities are defined and legitimated in quite discrepant ways, and the construction of an overarching world view that will embrace all of them becomes highly problematic. An important characteristic of the construction of symbolic universes under modern conditions is the sheer number of items that must be included in such a construct.

Sixth: *Progressivity*. There is a tendency to maximize the results or benefits of any action, a tendency that can be traced to the engineering mentality of technological production. This tendency produces a basic instability, expressed in the notion that "things can always be improved." Combined with the concept of "makeability," this leads to an "onward and upward" view of the world. There is not only an expectation of recurring and ongoing change but a positive attitude toward such change. Unfortunately, there is not room here to discuss the very interesting question as to whether or not this particular attitude may contradict some constitutionally given human characteristics.

Turning to bureaucracy, the most important themes for the overarching symbolic universe of modernity seem to be:

First: *The thematization of "society" itself*. Under a bureaucracy, society is experienced as an amorphous reality that has to be organized. It becomes both problematic and manageable—and it is understood to be manageable in different ways. Thus the phenomenon "society" emerges first as a system and second as a system to be tinkered with. There is a built-in principle of change and changeability very similar to the theme of "makeability" just discussed. This principle is always in tension, however, with the ordering propensity that accompanies what we have called the taxonomic style of bureaucratic consciousness. This view of society can be both comforting and burdensome, particularly since it contradicts the way in which social experience was defined through most of human history. This particular theme therefore frequently gives rise to fantasies and counterdesigns of different non-bureaucratic ways of life.

Second: *The thematization of bureaucracy and its taxonomic actions as a way of mitigating the threats of plurality.* The pluralization of social life means that the individual must constantly keep before him, and react to, a bewildering variety of experiences and elements of consciousness. Bureaucratic taxonomy is a way of ordering this variety. The bureaucratic notion of jurisdiction is blown up to become a kind of cosmic principle. Reality as a whole becomes amenable to bureaucratic ordering and, insofar as possible, to bureaucratic management. At the same time, the notion of jurisdiction derived from bureaucracy legitimates both plural social existences and role distance.[16]

"Role distance" means playing one's social roles "tongue in cheek" and maintaining both to oneself and to others that one's real identity is not comprehended by social roles. This is an overarching extension of the fundamental bureaucratic principle by which a bureaucrat acts "in office" qua bureaucrat, and qua bureaucrat *only*. It is simultaneously a defense against plurality *and* a pluralization of identity.

Third: *The "allocation" of particular jurisdictional space to the private sphere.* As we saw in the discussion of the pluralization of social life-worlds, this particular aspect of modernity is not derived *exclusively* from primary carriers, although it is closely related to them. But in whatever way the private sphere may relate to different institutional carriers, the cleavage between private and public spheres is a basic principle of modernity, on the level of both institutions and consciousness. Anti-modern ideologies are typically opposed to this cleavage, as we will have occasion to see in greater detail later.

Fourth: A further theme is *the notion of human rights being related to bureaucratically identifiable rights*, although it is not clear whether this is intrinsically or only extrinsically related to bureaucracy. *Some* bureaucracy is always supposed to be responsible for specific human rights. And it is assumed that there must always be somebody (and somebody who can be bureaucratically defined, therefore bureaucratically "found") to complain to. Related to this is a general theme stressing the importance of proper procedures,[17] which is closely related to the theme of the bureaucratic manageability of society. Thus there is a progression from the notion of universal human rights to the notion of a necessary universal bureaucracy. The United Nations may be seen as a somewhat ironic anticipation of this cosmological vision of bureaucracy. As we have observed before, such potentially cosmic extension seems to be intrinsic to the consciousness of bureaucracy. Talcott Parsons has described the difference between universalistic and particularistic pattern variables and has stressed that modernization typically involves a progression from particularism to universalism.[18] We would agree with this, but would add that under modern conditions particularism *presupposes* a universalistic context.

II

MODERNIZATION

On this dirty patch
a tree once stood
shedding incense on the infant corn:
its boughs stretched across a heaven
brightened by the last fires of a tribe.
They sent surveyors and builders
who cut that tree
planting in its place
A huge senseless cathedral of doom.

—KOFI AWOONOR

The Transmission of Packages

Modernization cannot be understood only as an institutional process, nor only as a movement on the level of consciousness. If it is to be grasped in its full impact, modernization must be regarded as a process by which specific clusters of institutions and contents of consciousness are transmitted. In the sense in which we have defined this term before, modernization is a process of transmission of packages. In this chapter we are concerned with the institutional vectors of this process.

We have emphasized that modern consciousness is an assemblage or constellation of specific themes. This means that although we have not introduced measures or scales, our approach has been "quantitative" rather than typological. In other words, we have tried to analyze modern consciousness in terms of a variety of cognitive and normative themes so that the degree of modernity could be gauged by the frequency and intensity of these themes. It follows that no society is ever modern in a total or exclusive sense, and few societies today can be described simply as non-modern. Rather, different societies show different frequencies and accumulations of the themes in question. Nevertheless there are sharp differences between the most advanced industrial societies and most societies of the so-called Third World. Although the former, which still contain within their own borders "pockets" of non-modern institutions and consciousness, have not completed the modernization process (and, as we will try to show in the third part of this book, may never complete it), they constitute centers from which this process radiates outward into less advanced societies. This, of course, is why modernization in much of the world today presents itself as a process of Westernization. As such, it is a process not only of social change but of cultural imposition. This section of the book is concerned with the manner in which such an imposition affects the societies of the Third World today.

The current process of modernization in the Third World is quite different from the processes by which societies reached modernity in the past. Not only are Third World societies latecomers to modernization, but the process has reached them, and to a large degree still reaches them, from the outside. For this reason it is important not to see contemporary Third World phenomena as more or less simple replications of what happened in Europe or North America in an earlier period.

The technological economic and bureaucratic political areas that we have found basic to modernity are indeed central in the Third World today. They do not, however, impinge equally or uniformly on all situations, and they are related to secondary carriers (such as education or urbanization) which often attain relative autonomy as modernizing agents.

We would therefore hypothesize that the degree of development of the technological economy is as much a key variant in the Third World as it is in the advanced industrial societies. Put in its simplest form, this would mean that there is a direct relationship between GNP and consciousness. However, the development of the economy in the direction of advanced technological production takes different forms, which have different consequences for both society and consciousness. This fact emerges quite clearly from the data on the effects of different work situations.

A very common pattern in the Third World is that the modern economy reaches into a situation in terms of various enterprises which require only small contingents of people with modern work attitudes. Most of the people in the situation, including most of the workers, are related to the enterprises in question by the performance of low-skill labor or not at all. Despite the modernity of a particular economic activity, it would be thoroughly obfuscating to look at such a situation simply in terms of modernization. What frequently happens in such cases is that there are very destructive effects on traditional patterns of life *without* any significant modernization of consciousness in terms of positively identifiable themes.

Mining is a good case in point. In southern Africa, mining has in many places been the activity that has represented the extension of a modern economy into a particular territory.[1] It has attracted large masses of African labor. Often, within a short time of the establishment of mining centers, streams of migrants move toward it. The immediate consequence is the weakening of village life and its traditional cultural patterns. In many cases the majority of male adults in a village migrate to the mining centers. While such migration often has serious effects on the communities left behind by the migrants, the effects on the migrants themselves are probably much more devastating. Individuals are torn out of the familiar protective structures of traditional life, in most cases physically separated from their families —becoming so-called industrial bachelors—and thrown into an amorphous and often chaotic mass of uprooted individuals organized rather remotely by plant management for purposes of labor.

In such a situation the structures of modernity (in terms of institutions, patterns of everyday life, cognitive and normative themes and anything else one may wish to name) must necessarily appear to the individual as an alien, powerful and, in the main, coercive force that completely uproots his life and the lives of those he most cares about. In such a situation there is little if any direct identification with modernity.

Such identification begins to grow with the length of time that an individual is exposed to the new situation. In the type of African situation just referred to, this transition is often externally expressed when workers are joined by their families.[2] In a literal sense the individual now "settles down" in the new situation and begins to come to terms with it in his everyday life. The data indicate that this process of accommodation has a cognitive side, as workers begin to understand at least some of the presuppositions that govern their work situation.[3] In the early stages of employment the African worker finds it difficult to understand the principles by which the enterprise is operated. For example, an African worker doing hard manual work, which in mining often involves serious dangers underground, is perplexed by a system which pays more money to men who sit in offices on a job which requires no physical strength and has no unusual hazards. As individuals move up in the hierarchy of labor, their understanding of this new valuation system progresses. Indeed, especially if they are successful in the new terms, they begin to identify with this way of looking at things.

A widespread prejudice in the West maintains that non-Western cultures discourage work and even produce individuals with an inherent incapacity for it. The data do not support this. There is widespread evidence that people in just about every area of the world have the capacity to work systematically and well, to be trained in modern methods of work and to acquire high degrees of technological skill.[4] We are also skeptical of the more sophisticated view that non-Western cultures do not encourage the need for achievement.[5] It seems to us much more in accordance with the evidence to say that non-Western cultures operate in *different frames of reference* with regard to conceptions of work *and* of achievement. Indeed, even the cursory traveler in Latin America or in Africa is often impressed by the capacity of people for hard, sustained and disciplined work. This work, however, moves in rhythms different from those the Western traveler is accustomed to, and its meaning appears to be understood in a different way. Similarly, the objectives and motives of achievement differ. The problem of modernization in the area of production is not to get people to work, but to get them to work in a particular way. This involves the imposition not only of external patterns of activity but, equally important, of specific structures of consciousness. Until identification with the latter has taken place in the consciousness of the individual, the external patterns are perceived as alien and essentially meaningless. As long as the new patterns are not internalized (that is, integrated within the individual's subjective structures of consciousness), they "sit on" the individual in a loose and superficial manner, and his adherence to them is haphazard and unreliable. Adherence in one context can be only imperfectly transferred to another context. What is more, the individual easily "forgets" the whole thing—for example, if he returns to his traditional setting.[6]

In the initial stages of modernization in the economic area, only a small number of individuals become "modern types."[7] These are the people who first internalize the cognitive and normative themes intrinsic to a modern economy. Very often they are marginal types,[8] individuals who either for personal reasons or because of their adherence to a particular group have not been fully integrated into the life of the traditional community. They may be people who, because of this or that biographical accident, are "maladjusted" in their original social contexts. Or they may belong to ethnic, religious or class groups that place them on the fringes of the community. In terms of the traditional community, they represent cases of "imperfect socialization" on the levels of both overt activity and consciousness. By the same token, they are more prepared than others for socialization into the new patterns. In many cases this readiness to internalize new structures is no doubt sparked by the additional motive of resentment against the old.

Very commonly, the process of economic modernization begins in a highly compartmentalized fashion. A modern economy reaches its tentacles into a previously untouched region. Its initial impact is likely to be more destructive than constructive in terms of the patterns of everyday social life. Initially, only a few individuals or small groups identify with the process. The longer it lasts, however, the more likely it is that its patterns will spread and be effectively internalized by larger numbers of people.

Each phase in the establishment of modern economic institutions has its correlate on the level of consciousness. Thus, for example, the substitution of a modern cash economy for a traditional barter system not only revolutionizes economic transactions but necessitates cognitive innovation as well.[9] As payments are made in cash rather than in kind, new notions of measurability become internalized. New elements of impersonality and formality are introduced into social relations. New institutions, such as credit associations, arise as mediators in this process.[10] But something even more important takes place at the same time—the economic sphere begins to be perceived as an independent and highly specific area of human life.[11] It comes to be taken for granted that economic transactions entail assumptions and rules that are sharply distinct from those that govern other activities in social life. One of the most distinctive features of modernity, the dichotomization between the public and private spheres, comes to be internalized in consciousness. Rationality and impersonality come to be experienced not simply as alien impositions but as necessary and perhaps even beneficial criteria dominating at least the economic sphere. Later we will touch upon the various possibilities of these themes being carried over from the economic sphere to other sectors of social life.

This suggests that there are a number of crucial variants to be looked at in connection with the transmission of modernizing packages by means of economic carriers. First, there is the type of modern economic activity entering a particular situation. This involves such questions as the kind of labor skills it requires, the degree to which it makes use of indigenous labor in the job hierarchy, the size of the enterprise in question and its relationship to other economic activities (both traditional and modern) in the area. Second, there is the length of time that a modern or modernizing economic activity has been present in a particular area. As we have seen, whatever may be the effects of an economic enterprise on social life and consciousness, these effects are strengthened and deepened with the passage of time. Both these variants refer to economic activity in relation to broad macro-social contexts. Whatever the macro-social situation may be, it is also possible to approach the matter in terms of a third variant, the relationship of particular individuals to the modernizing economic activity. Both the unskilled miner and the executive trainee in, let us say, an African country, are related to a modernizing activity. But the two relationships are drastically different. Needless to say, there is an exceedingly intricate variety of such individual relationships. It is therefore not enough to say that in a particular situation macro-social forces of modernization are at work in the economic sphere (or for that matter in any other sphere of social life). It is necessary to analyze the manner in which particular individuals or groups relate to the modernizing carriers. In terms of our own theoretical presuppositions we will assume (or, more accurately, hypothesize) that each such relationship has its specific correlate on the level of consciousness.

The other principal carrier of modernization, along with the institutions of technologized economy, is the bureaucratic state. To some extent, of course, the variants just discussed in connection with the economy also apply to the state. The type of bureaucratic structure (for example, civilian as against military), its size, the length of time it has been in a particular situation and the different ways in which individuals relate to it are all variants that must be taken into account in any analysis. Nevertheless, there are some very important differences between the economic and political carriers of modernization.[12]

Both the modern state and the modern economy impose themselves as alien realities upon traditional social situations. In the early stages of this process, and even later on, most people in the situation may see little difference in the manner in which these two institutional complexes are perceived and experienced. An important difference emerges later, however, particularly in politically independent countries (such as the new states of Africa or revolutionary regimes in Latin America or Asia): the state presents itself as a mobilizing agent for development and as a symbol of all-important collective aspirations. This makes it easier for people, especially the emerging "modern types," to identify with the state rather than the economic system, and to regard it as a vehicle of their social ambitions instead of an inhibiting structure. For example, data on Africa indicate that government employment has far greater attraction for upwardly mobile young people than employment in economic enterprises.[13] Careers in the government bureaucracy are perceived as being both more glamorous and less strenuous. Indeed, the government bureaucracy and its career ladder appear as the road leading to the pinnacle of status, privilege and power.

This is probably because the bureaucracy is able to accommodate itself to traditional patterns of social relations more easily than an increasingly technological economy can. Even a very modern bureaucratic structure can establish working relations with traditional power structures far better than a modern economic enterprise can with traditional patterns of production. Traditional patterns can actually be incorporated into the workings of the bureaucracy, as the importance of family, clan and tribal loyalties in the politics of Third World states clearly indicates.[14]

This "mix" between modern and traditional patterns in the area of the state go far to explain the greater ease with which people can identify with the state. But another element is involved too, an element very close indeed to the perception of the situation involved in the data on employment preferences. It is indeed "easier" to climb a political career ladder than an economic one. Fewer skills are or seem to be involved. Especially in times of rapid political change, an individual can be catapulted almost instantaneously from the lower to the highest reaches of the system. Thus one must take into account here not only the imagery of power but very real objective possibilities of power.

At the same time, however, there are significant illusions related to these perceptions. The principal one is that power requires no special skills. One may be skeptical about this perception in any society, including a traditional one, but it is a patent illusion applied to a modern or modernizing society. Such a society must necessarily be administered bureaucratically. Bureaucracy entails not only very specific skills but, as we have tried to show, a very specific structure of consciousness. These skills and this consciousness must be acquired in a learning process that very often is arduous and slow—in other words, a learning process that is diametrically opposed to the expectations just described. The result of this conflict between institutional requirements and subjective expectations is simple but far-reaching: in many Third World societies we see bureaucratic structures operated on all levels by people who have only imperfectly, or sometimes not at all, internalized the structures of consciousness on which a bureaucracy depends.

This illusion about the nature of political power not only is current among those within the bureaucratic structure but communicates itself to the bureaucracy's clients as well. In an interesting and perhaps paradoxical way, some of our previous observations on the structures of consciousness of bureaucracy are relevant here. We tried to show that unlike the structures of consciousness pertaining to technological production, bureaucracy entails *discrepant frames of reference* as between its practitioners and its clients. In other words, the client of bureaucracy does not have to enter into the bureaucrat's frame of reference in order to interact with him. But the worker in technological production must, at least to a certain degree, share the same frame of reference as the engineer who devised the particular production process in order to participate in it effectively. This is relevant to the modernizing situation. While, as we have seen, it is possible for workers to relate to a modern economic enterprise with minimal or no participation in its ethos or cognitive system, such participation grows with time. There need be no such growth in participation in the case of bureaucracy. This may mean quite simply that large numbers of people continue to expect wonders from the state without in the least understanding the mechanisms that would be necessary to bring these wonders about.

At the same time they can identify with the glamorous symbols of political power. As with all symbols of power, political or religious, throughout human history, identification without understanding is very possible—indeed it might be argued that identification is easier without such understanding. An exhilarated identification with new symbols of state power can occur almost instantaneously. An understanding of the efforts required to make a new state into a viable entity is a different matter altogether. Thus in eastern Africa, particularly in Kenya and Tanzania, the political leadership has made great efforts to educate people in the necessary linkage between *uhuru* (independence) and *kazi* (work), emphasizing that the former will become hollow and transitory without the latter. It can be safely asserted that *uhuru* has enjoyed considerably greater popularity among the masses of the people than *kazi* has. Again, it would be a serious mistake to attribute this to some intrinsic aversion to work in these particular societies. The failure is of imagination rather than of morality. The work required to make a modern African state viable economically and politically requires extensive modifications of traditional ways of doing things and of understanding the world. By contrast, the symbols of national sovereignty and state power are or seem to be immediately accessible to the imagination. Needless to say, this accessibility is deliberately fostered by governments that base themselves upon a strongly nationalistic ideology.

The sociological consequences of the foregoing considerations are very far-reaching indeed. We will mention only two. First, in modernizing societies today the political carrier of modernization generally appears to be more important than the economic one—appears to be so, that is, in the minds of the people in the situation. While there is undoubtedly a realistic component to this perception, there are also important elements of illusion. Second, in most modernizing societies today a specifically political middle class has emerged—that is, a relatively educated and privileged stratum which derives its position mainly from employment in the state bureaucratic apparatus.

The social dynamics of such a middle class are quite different from those that produced the bourgeoisie in Western countries. It is not enough to say that its consciousness is shaped by political rather than economic institutions. More importantly, its conception of modernization is shaped considerably more by the structures of bureaucratic consciousness than by those of technological production. It is the imagination of the politician and the bureaucrat that are of paramount importance in shaping most Third World societies—not the imagination of the engineer or the economic entrepreneur. Implicit in this is a strong tendency toward socialism, which must be added as a causal factor to a number of other factors that propel many Third World societies in a socialist direction. We shall have occasion to return to this point a little later.

The other institutional vectors of modernization enumerated in the preceding chapter may be covered briefly. One is the cultural location of the primary carriers, and here it must be emphasized again that an essential difference between Third World societies today and the process of modernization in Western societies earlier is that today the impulse for modernization comes from outside the cultures in question. To a large extent, modernization in the Third World has been tantamount to Westernization, both in objective social fact and in the subjective perceptions of the people affected. In these countries the economic and political carriers were alien importations. Needless to say, this fact has been one of the great energizing motives in the development of Asian, African and even Latin American nationalism (though in the last case the animus of nationalism has been directed against the United States rather than the West, since Latin American cultures have been Western at least "officially" for a long time).

Nationalism often obscures the alien character of the modernizing agencies. And a universal aspiration of nationalist movements in the Third World and of the independent states created in the wake of colonialism has been to make government *less* alien to the people. To some extent the effort has succeeded. The simple fact of national independence or the establishment of a national government apparatus does not, however, automatically bring government closer to the people. Data from India indicate that the establishment of an Indian national government, and even of state governments, has not appreciably changed the people's perception of government as an alien entity in village India.[15]

This is because in most traditional societies the significant unit of social identification is the village or the tribe rather than any larger unit. From the point of view of an Indian villager, the national government of India is as remote as the British Raj was. To a slightly lesser degree, this is also true of state government. Indian data show villagers turning away from modern political institutions and establishing their own forms of leadership (like the traditional caste council) to counteract the agencies of modern government. Similar data are available from Africa, where tribal and ethnic identifications have, if anything, increased since the end of the colonial era.[16]

These facts are particularly galling to nationalist intellectuals who perceive themselves as being closely linked to the people at large. In this perception they tend to overlook the degree of their own Westernization and therefore the degree to which they themselves appear as outsiders to the traditional elements in their own society. Indeed, there are data from Tunisia that indicate that traditional villages are more suspicious of middle-class intellectuals from their national capital than they are of Europeans.[17]

The cultural location of the modernizing agencies makes a very great difference to the portion of the population that has been subjected to a considerable degree of Western education.[18] In recently colonial countries the vivid memory of discrimination against indigenous personnel in political and economic institutions still remains. Even in countries where such memories are fading, resentment against the West is a powerful motivating force among the educated classes. This resentment may be increased by the often unadmitted recognition that while the West and all its works are violently rejected, the nation's goals of development and modernization cannot be achieved without accepting at least a measure of Westernization and of Western-derived institutions. The aim of many nationalist ideologies in the Third World is to resolve this cognitive discrepancy. Typically, this takes the form of continuing to reject what are designated as the undesirable characteristics of Western culture while being willing to adopt and adapt those elements that are deemed necessary and desirable. Among the latter, modern technology and its applications in the economic sphere rank very high. Once more, there is a strong tendency toward socialism. Indeed, if one explores the actual cognitive content of such ideologies as "African socialism" or "Arab socialism," one finds that the reconciliation of discrepancy is crucial.[19] Western culture, particularly in its West European and North American forms of capitalism, is perceived as a social system that not only exploits people but also atomizes society and uproots the individual. By contrast, the new socialism (which is only rarely akin to socialism in any sector of the advanced industrial world) is seen as a system that will combine the benefits of modernity with a community that offers the individual both meaning and solidarity. A more important vector of modernization is access to the economic benefits of modernity. Most national societies today are related to modern economic processes and to the international system these processes constitute. The nature of the relationship differs vastly, however, in different countries. Most countries of the Third World are overwhelmingly poor, and most of their people have only minimal access to the economic benefits of modernity, as compared with the people in advanced industrial societies. Marxist analysts of this situation have focused on economic dependency as the basic feature of underdevelopment and have argued that underdevelopment itself is a direct result of exploitation.[20] We are skeptical of this type of analysis if it is made into a generalized explanation. The causes of underdevelopment are far more complex, and exploitation of Third World countries by more advanced economies is only one of many features in the situation, although in the case of certain countries it may well be the predominant one. But there can be no difference of opinion on the pervasive reality of poverty in most societies of the Third World.

This poverty has both objective and subjective elements. There are the objective facts of underdevelopment and the conditions of life it creates. On the level of everyday experience, there are the massive realities of hunger, disease and early death. But the same facts have a subjective side, and in order to understand what is going on in the Third World today it is necessary to look at both elements of the situation. Poverty and, indeed, dependency and exploitation are not simply objective facts to be uncovered by the economist or the political scientist. They are also definitions of the situation and elements of consciousness.

Even in its initial phases, modernization entails an expansion of the individual's social horizon.[21] Through education and mass communication, and also through face-to-face contact with individual agents of the primary modernization carriers, the individual becomes conscious of a world beyond the confines of his everyday social experience. Inevitably, he begins to compare his own situation with that world. Almost inevitably, the comparison is depressing insofar as the new horizon includes information and imagery about advanced industrial societies. What previously was perceived as being part of the human condition and its destiny now comes to be perceived as a very particular condition, an unjust one, and one that at least in principle might be changed. For these reasons there is a widespread and, we believe, increasing linkage between modernization and the rise of social dissatisfaction and revolutionary consciousness. This linkage would probably emerge by itself, in view of the aforementioned situation, but it has been greatly furthered by political movements that have the express purpose of fostering revolution and that quite correctly understand revolutionary consciousness as the necessary prerequisite for any far-reaching transformation of these societies.

It is here that our analysis links up with what Marxists in Latin America have come to call "conscientization,"[22] that is, the deliberate use of education and political propaganda to make people conscious of the social and political determinants of their situation, particularly their own exploitation, so that they are ready to act politically. The linkage of modernization with revolutionary consciousness is important not only for political movements that seek to overthrow existing regimes but also for nationalist governments that plan to mobilize their populations for purposes of development. But even if many of the structures of consciousness transmitted in such situations are similar to the packages transmitted in politically less volatile circumstances, the emotional style differs greatly in the two cases. Where mobilization is successful (be it mobilization for revolution or for the postrevolutionary consolidation of a new regime), every aspect of modernization is perceived as an instrument of liberation (or rather is so perceived if this particular aspect is part of the revolutionary program). At least for certain periods of time, this permits very rapid modernization while preserving the individual's sense of community. It is therefore not surprising that revolutionary "conscientization" is widely employed by regimes that want to mobilize their populations for rapid development.[23] The advantages of such mobilization are obvious. The major risk is what happens when, after expectations and enthusiasm have been roused to a fever pitch, the goals of development are not reached. The case of Cuba is very instructive in this regard.[24]

The institutional vector that we have called the social organization of the economy reduces itself, for all practical purposes, to the question of capitalist versus socialist models of modernization. Modernization along broadly capitalist lines tends to produce a highly restless, insecure population. Those whose lives have been uprooted by the modernizing processes (such as those who have been forced off the land or attracted to the cities) commonly find themselves in a threatening situation and, what is more, without legitimations for this situation. Such people are attracted by political movements that promise a radical change in their circumstances and, simultaneously, personal security in return for total commitment. We doubt whether the dislocations involved in modernization are necessarily less harsh if the economy is organized along socialist lines. A socialist system, however, provides clearly defined goals, both collectively and individually, and thus legitimates the dislocations as necessary steps on the path to full development. We are not concerned here with the question of whether capitalist or socialist models of development are more appropriate for the Third World. Nor should our observations be taken as an argument in favor of socialism. All we say is that there are very strong *non-economic* reasons why socialism in one form or another presents itself as the more attractive model in an increasing number of Third World countries. These non-economic factors must be taken into account, no matter how one estimates the economic plausibility of socialist as against capitalist models of development.

We are not speaking here of socialism in terms of Marxist ideology. To prevent such a misunderstanding, let us look at the military as an agent of modernization.[25] Whatever the political role of the military in this or that country, its function as a modernizing agent *for the individual* is essentially socialist. While the individual who enters the military is uprooted from his traditional setting and subjected to fundamental accommodations to modernity under highly coercive controls, he is also the beneficiary of important compensations for these deprivations. He is provided with a new status and, to the extent that he internalizes it, a new identity. His life is given form and meaning in a group with a high degree of solidarity. His future can be clearly visualized and is presented to him, at least in part, as dependent upon his own efforts. In this context, the military has shown itself to be one of the most successful agents of modernization, including most especially the modernization of consciousness. Within the military, individuals are introduced to the possibility of shaping their own future. There are predictable relationships between effort and reward, and most important, there is a system of equity based on merit. It is therefore hardly surprising that a number of Third World countries have come to be ruled by military regimes.

In the first part of this book we repeatedly emphasized that the dichotomization of private and public life is one of the crucial social characteristics of modernity. Modernization in contemporary Third World societies imposes this same dichotomization, and in most instances it is felt to be an extremely difficult and often repugnant ordeal,[26] which gives birth to profound threats of anomie. Socialism presents itself as a solution to this problem. It promises to reintegrate the individual in all-embracing structures of solidarity. *If modernization can be described as a spreading condition of homelessness, then socialism can be understood as the promise of a new home.*

A final institutional vector, the degree of bureaucratic autonomy, can be directly related to what has just been said. For many reasons, only some of which have been discussed here, the state and its apparatus occupy a central position in most contemporary Third World societies. The tendency toward socialism further intensifies this centralization. Both the expectations of collective betterment (that is, the expectations of development) and the hopes of the individual tend to be attached to the state and its political promises. This situation is not conducive to pluralization of power or even to restraints upon the autonomy of the bureaucratic apparatus.

6

Collisions of Consciousness

In the countries commonly referred to as the Third World, modernity is a powerful vision full of images, some glittering with promise, others ominously threatening. And today this vision fills the lives of an increasing number of people in the world. Even more important, since modernity is seen as the wave of the future, the vision looms ahead on the horizon into which life seems to be moving.

A great many personal and collective expectations are attached to the vision of modernity, not all of them positive. Yet on the most elementary levels of human experience, modernity is associated with the expectation of being delivered from hunger, disease and early death. Thus modernity has about it a quality of miracle and magic which, in some instances, can link up with old religious expectations of delivery from the sufferings of the human condition. But it is safe to assume that the imagery

of modernity is almost never limited simply to these ele-
mental expectations. Through various means of communication a stock of knowledge about the modern world is
widely diffused. This includes information (sometimes
reliable, sometimes not) about the character of advanced
industrial societies, as well as information about what is
going on in one's own society and prognoses as to that
society's future. Such communication takes place even
when direct contact with modernizing forces is very limited. The mass media, especially the transistor radio and
the motion picture, reach into territories that have been
barely touched by the primary carriers of modernization.
But even more important, communication is spread by
hearsay. There are always people who have been somewhere else—in some nearby town, or in the capital city
or perhaps even abroad. Such individuals, when they return to their own community, become important disseminators of this kind of information and perspective.

A very instructive illustration of the way in which
this kind of communication can powerfully affect areas
quite marginal to the major modernization processes may
be found in Jean Duvignaud's study of Shebika, a village
in Tunisia.[1] As Duvignaud describes the village, it has
remained virtually untouched by the technological, economic and political agents of modernization. Yet the village is affected by a steady stream of modernizing communication. There is a school, and most of the younger
children can read. Thus they become the possessors and
disseminators of a variety of facts about the outside world.
There are also in the village a number of individuals who
served in the French or Tunisian armies, some of them
abroad. They too are important informants concerning the
modern world. Finally, there are a number of transistor
radios, to which Duvignaud gives an important place

among the influences that have changed the character of village life.

Duvignaud shows how a situation can be drastically affected by communication of this sort, *even if nothing else changes*—and in this particular case *precisely because* nothing else changes. The new lore disseminated by the schoolchildren, the stories of faraway places told by the army veterans, and the steady barrage of information and propaganda (especially propaganda by the Tunisian government following that country's independence) coming over the radio have all had one major consequence: the expectations of life have changed in Shebika. The villagers were particularly roused to higher expectations by promises made by politicians and government officials over the radio. They expected the government to do very concrete things to improve their situation, such as providing building materials to repair their houses. When these expectations remained unfulfilled, there was mounting frustration and anger. This finally led to a critical confrontation with representatives of the government, a confrontation that came very close to a rebellion.

The new images of modernity inevitably collide with the symbols, values and beliefs of traditional society. To anyone with a personal commitment to the tradition in question this collision constitutes a potent threat. One of Duvignaud's villagers expressed himself as follows ("Sidi Sultan" refers to a local Muslim shrine): "Nothing's left, nothing. When people come, we let them make an offering. Why not? But Sidi Sultan no longer answers their prayers. The old ways are gone; the bonds are loosened. We go through the motions, but what of it? ... The radio has killed everything."[2]

Yet to others in such a situation, modernity appears as images of glittering allure. Daniel Lerner, in his study of social change in the Middle East, presents a portrait of the grocer in a Turkish village, a man who welcomed modernity and who was himself an agent of modernization.[3] In one conversation with Lerner's researchers, the grocer described in some detail what he would like his store to look like eventually. The description given in glowing terms was that of an American supermarket. Affluence, technical marvels, consumer choice, the sense of benefiting from the achievements of progress—all these elements are present in this Turkish fantasy of an A&P.

In most of the Third World the allure of modernity is strongly linked to city life. It is for this reason, quite apart from the promise of economic opportunity, that the city serves as such a powerful magnet. To be sure, people migrate there in the expectation of finding better employment and better material conditions of life. Yet these often highly rational expectations are coupled with something else that is almost mystical in character. This is the mystique of modernity, which has its most powerful manifestation in the city. The rational expectations are disappointed more often than not. The fastest-growing type of urban agglomeration in the Third World is the slum. The hopes for good jobs, better housing or better health most frequently come to a cruel end in the *favelas* of Latin America, the *bidonvilles* of Africa and the shanty-towns of Asia. The mystique, however, tends to be stronger than the rational expectations. *It survives the disappointment of the latter.* Whatever its frustrations and degradations, the city continues to be the place where things are happening, where there is movement and a sense of the future. The mystique gives proof of its durability very clearly when, coupled with the resentment and anger of shattered dreams, it transforms itself into revolutionary consciousness.

The symbols of modernity, and with them the entire vision of the modern world, are not simply diffused in a haphazard manner. Often they are deliberately manipulated, for either economic or political reasons. In those areas of the Third World that continue to be penetrated by capitalist enterprise, such manipulation is undertaken by advertising. It is not, needless to say, terribly different from the manipulation undertaken by advertising in advanced industrial societies of North America or Western Europe. In the Third World, however, it has a much greater impact because it links up directly with sometimes desperate expectations of a better life, and also because it imposes itself on a population that is much less sophisticated with regard to the deceptions of this form of communication. The Coca-Cola sign erected on the edge of a poverty-stricken village in some Third World country has become a notorious example of this type of manipulation. The manipulation can also be political, however, and in this form it is employed by Third World governments regardless of the manner in which their economy is organized. A villager in Latin America may be symbolically manipulated by advertising agencies in the employment of the producers of Coca-Cola, or by propaganda outlets of the regime of Fidel Castro. Whatever else may be different, as between these two types of manipulation, they have one very important thing in common: *both* are related to the mystique of modernity and its promise of a better life. Conversely, *both* are inimical to the traditional patterns of village life.

The governments of newly independent countries of the Third World have often been chastised by Western observers for their lavish expenditures on purely symbolic enterprises. The erection of magnificent government buildings in the capital city, or the establishment of a national airline, are favorite cases in point. The Western observers in question habitually point out that the governments cannot afford such expenditures. In purely economic terms this may be true. Men, however, do not live by bread alone—especially not in situations of desperate need and urgent hope. In such situations men at least *also* live on dreams. To the extent that this is true, one may say that many of these governments cannot afford *not* to manipulate symbols in these or comparable ways. The magnificent new buildings in the capital city and the powerful new airplanes that bear the national colors are not simply, and sometimes not at all, the result of rational economic calculations. Rather, they are symbols, indeed, one may say, *sacraments of modernity and its promises*. They confirm the plausibility of the vision, and they serve as a visible token of the government's commitment to the realization of all the hopes that are linked to the vision.

The symbols of modernity are not only diffused through the mass media of communication, but they also have important embodiments on the level of everyday life. To take two important examples, the place of the wristwatch and the ballpoint pen in the Third World today cannot be understood simply in functional, utilitarian terms. These objects are above all symbolic. They symbolize the modern status of the individual who owns and exhibits them, and they are well chosen indeed. The one refers to literacy and the immense new stock of knowledge that literacy opens up, the other, to that structure of time which, as we tried to show earlier, lies at the very roots of modern technological production and modern bureaucracy, and thus of modern society as such. As the symbols of modernity are visibly attached to the human body, so are modern structures of consciousness superimposed upon the human mind. Again, the significance of wristwatch and ballpoint pen can be put in sacramental terms. They are the outward, visible signs of an inward transformation of consciousness. They express the collisions, the conflicts and even the rituals brought about by the intrusions of modernity into traditional social life.[4]

As modernization proceeds, there is a transformation both in the organization of knowledge and in cognitive style, in what is known and in how it is known. The transformation in the organization of knowledge is illustrated by one of Duvignaud's respondents as he expounds the traditional point of view in these matters: "All knowledge belongs to God, and it is divided into two parts: hidden knowledge and visible knowledge. Hidden knowledge was hidden by God, and it has five parts: lawmaking, benevolence, rain, spirits and *jinn*. Visible knowledge has three parts: politics, charity and the knowledge of Satan. The knowledge of Satan has four subdivisions: the knowledge of Satan proper, the politics of philosophy, geometry and industry. But these last four exist only in Europe."[5] This particular conversation is about the village school. To make clear just how ambivalent the respondent's conception of "the knowledge of Satan" is, it is worth following the conversation a little further. The researcher goes on to ask, "So geometry and philosophy belong to the knowledge of Satan?" The respondent replies, "Industry and geometry are for those who have denied their religion." Logically enough, the researcher inquires, "Do you think that the young people who have been to school should stay here or should go away?" The reply to this question is: "If they can go, let them go."

The organization of knowledge as articulated by a traditional Tunisian villager is, of course, highly specific and may bear little resemblance to the organization of knowledge in other traditional societies. But the new organization of knowledge brought about by modernization is very similar indeed all over the world, for the reasons that we have already discussed. The new bodies of knowledge come into traditional societies as invading armies. Reality is redefined and reclassified in almost every sector of social life.

As we have indicated before, the initial effect of this invasion is almost invariably a sense of disorientation and of loss in the consciousness of the individuals involved. With the social presence of new bodies of knowledge there is also a new social distribution of knowledge. Different individuals and groups have different access to the new bodies of knowledge. This may have far-reaching, cataclysmic consequences. In a society in which wisdom used to be associated with old age there may be a sudden reversal as the young and the very young can plausibly present themselves as privileged interpreters of the mysteries of modernity. In such situations the dethroned elders naturally have rather mixed feelings about the change.

As with any organization of knowledge, there are experts and nonexperts. Modernization legitimates new experts and simultaneously de-legitimates old ones. Some of this legitimation may be informal, as, for example, when the homecoming migrant suddenly acquires prestige as the man who has experienced and can tell about the mysteries of the great city. But there are also highly formal and institutionalized processes by which the new experts are legitimated. The most important of these legitimating agencies is the school.[6] Quite apart from the degree of information or skill actually transmitted by the school in a modernizing situation, its very presence serves to legitimate the new bodies of knowledge, and to bestow status upon those who have begun in whatever measure to acquire the new lore. Ivan Illich has very aptly called the school "the new universal church." The "religion" proclaimed by this new church is the mystique of modernity. As with the old church, the ritual representing the new mysteries need not be comprehensible to the people at large. Indeed, it may be argued that something is gained by incomprehensibility. In other words, it is not at all necessary that the lore transmitted by the school be coherent, let alone useful. The children mumbling away in the schoolhouse are engaged in a ritual very similar to that of the priest and his helpers around the altar. The congregation watches and stands in awe. It is not at all necessary that it understand the Latin.

Profound transformations also take place in cognitive style. Although we cannot discuss here the question of whether, despite the great variety of traditional cultures, there may be what the Dutch historian Jan Romein has called the "common human pattern" from which modernity constitutes an abrupt deviation,[7] there is no doubt that comparable collisions between modern and traditional elements of cognitive style may be observed in different parts of the world. Most important, the specific form of rationality associated with modern science, technology and technologized economy imposes itself as an alien force in most traditional societies. It redefines reality as an object of deliberate, systematic and rational human activity. By contrast, consider this description by a French psychologist of what he claims to be a general African attitude toward the world: "Thus the world in its entirety appears as consisting of a single tissue. Man cannot exercise domination over it by virtue of his spirit. What is more, this world is sacralized, and man must be prudent in the use he makes of it. All this is not very favorable to the development of economic relations that are purely objective. In such a world it is not certain that man can create riches: he must act in this world as a guest and not as an exploiting proprietor."[8] The last sentence succinctly states the fundamental opposition: man as guest and man as exploiter in the universe. As we tried to show earlier, this particular collision is most relevant to the structures of consciousness intrinsic to technological production—and by extension to any structures of consciousness that are directly or indirectly derived from this process.

There are a few other traditional patterns whose collisions with the structures of modern consciousness have wide import. One of these is the conception of reality as a living and generally interconnected fabric of beings. To quote again from the aforementioned African study: "No being exists by itself. All remain tied to the totality of things and in particular to those that have engendered them. It follows that individualism is strongly limited. No being and no object can be perfectly isolated, and every action is susceptible to lead to almost infinite consequences."[9] This kind of world view is in sharp opposition to the specifically modern pattern that we have called componentiality. As modern technological rationality penetrates a traditional society, the archaic unity of being is broken. The cosmic connection between all beings and all objects is severed. Reality is organized into components that can be apprehended and manipulated in isolation. To the extent that componentiality extends even to the realm of social relations and to the individual's experience of himself, it tends to be experienced as uprooting and alienating.

A basic element in any cognitive style is temporality, that is, the manner in which time is apprehended in consciousness. Both modern technology and modern bureaucracy presuppose temporal structures that are precise, highly quantifiable, universally applicable and, perhaps most important of all, capable of spanning past, present and future within the same categories. The last of these characteristics is particularly important in terms of actions projected into the future. Modernity runs of necessity on the time that can be measured on a wristwatch. This type of temporality is drastically alien to the overwhelming majority of traditional societies in the Third World, and quite possibly to all of them. John Mbiti, a contemporary African philosopher, maintains that traditional African consciousness lacks the category of the future as it has developed in Western thought. Time is divided into those events that have occurred in the past, those that are taking place right now or in the immediate future and those that inevitably and recurringly take place in the rhythms of natural phenomena. Whatever does not fit into these three categories is not apprehended as time at all. Rather, it is "no-time." As Mbiti explains: "The most significant consequence of this is that, according to traditional concepts, time is a two-dimensional phenomenon, with a long *past*, a *present*, and virtually *no future*. The linear concept of time in Western thought, with an indefinite past, present and infinite future, is practically foreign to African thinking. The future is virtually absent because events that lie in it have not taken place, they have not been realized, and cannot, therefore, constitute time. If, however, future events are certain to occur, or if they fall within the inevitable rhythm of nature, they at best constitute only *potential time*, not *actual time*. What is taking place now no doubt unfolds the future, but once an event has taken place, it is no longer in the future but in the present and the past. *Actual time* is therefore what is present and what is past. It moves 'backward' rather than 'forward'; and people set their minds not on future things, but chiefly on what has taken place."[10]

Such a conception of time is not restricted to Africa. It is, to say the least, widely diffused throughout Asia, and in the great Asian civilizations it was articulated in highly sophisticated philosophical systems. Whatever the Western notions of intellectual elites, a very similar conception of time is deeply embedded in Latin American cultures and to this day determines the social life of vast numbers of people in Latin America. With the onset of modernization, the specifically modern modes of temporality are superimposed on the earlier temporal structures on a number of different levels. Everyday social life is reorganized. In a traditional Mexican village, a *campesino* making an appointment would find it perfectly adequate to say, "I will see you in the evening." This might mean any time between, say, eight and eleven P.M. The modernized individual (at least if he is really concerned with keeping the appointment) is more likely to say "I will see you at nine-thirty." It hardly needs to be emphasized that such a change entails a profound transformation of the fabric of everyday life. The *campesino* will typically experience this transformation as a very disagreeable matter. He is likely to agree that it makes for more efficiency (a quality that he more readily attributes to North Americans than to himself), but at the same time he will feel that it leads to a rushed and harassing way of life that is inherently less humane than the traditional one.

This collision between different modes of temporality is inevitable within the confines of modern technological or bureaucratic activities. Thus it is clearly very difficult, if not impossible, to run a government office effectively on the time structure of the *campesino*. (It has often been argued that the recurring tendency to do so has much to do with the widespread inefficiency of government operations in the Third World.) The substitution of a modern time structure for a traditional one becomes particularly important in terms of planning. We need not repeat here our analysis of the life-planning of individuals and families in a modern society. Suffice it to say that such life-planning becomes increasingly diffused as modernization proceeds. In the process it necessarily collides with the traditional ways of apprehending the stages of biography. The same, of course, goes for planning on a societal scale. It would be very difficult indeed to plan economic production in terms of African "no-time," as it would be for a government to carry through a five-year plan within the time consciousness of traditional India. Thus the wristwatch is closely linked to the calendar—and not just to the calendar of the current year but to that of the coming decade or beyond.

Modernization also brings with it new typifications of others and of the individual's relations to them. Every society has some sort of operating typology to classify its members. At the least, there are types for age and sex groupings, and for different categories in the division of labor. In most societies, of course, the typology is far more complex. Modernization entails reclassification, often of a drastic and violent sort. William Hinton, in his study of the coming of the Communist revolution to a Chinese village, has described in great detail the manner in which the Communists reclassified the population for purposes of dealing with different groups of people.[11] The major relevant categories were those of rich peasants, middle peasants and poor peasants. It was of very great importance to the people in question whether they were put in one or the other of these categories. Indeed, in certain instances, classification determined life or death.

Depending upon the gyrations in the Party line, the criteria for classification were changed a number of times. Thus a person classified as a rich peasant at one point might mercifully be allowed to lapse into the category of middle peasant at another stage. Or, if the Party line was hardening, the opposite reclassification might occur. What Hinton is describing here is, of course, a process by which social reality is abruptly reclassified by the application of political and physical power. Aptly enough, Hinton's study is entitled *Fanshen*, a Chinese word meaning a complete turnabout in the order of things.

Similarly drastic reorderings of social relations are typical in the wake of successful revolutions. It would be a mistake, however, to limit one's conception of such *fanshen* to situations comparable to that of the Chinese revolution. In a less planned way *every* process of modernization entails *fanshen*. The phenomenon that in Africa has been called "detribalization" is essentially a similar process of radical social reclassification.[12] While traditionally one's fellow-men were classified in terms of tribal affiliations, these now are overlaid by completely different social typologies. Economic status, occupation, political party affiliation or urban neighborhood now vie with tribe as relevant criteria for grouping people. Declassification and reclassification go hand in hand in this process.

Because of very fundamental processes in social psychology, new typifications of others necessarily lead to new typifications of self. In other words, as the individual's apprehension of the social world is changed by modernization, so is his apprehension of his own identity. If, for example, it no longer makes sense for him to identify others in terms of tribe only, it will sooner or later make no sense for him to do so in his own case. Similarly, the reclassification of others in terms of a revolutionary ideology ipso facto includes a reclassification of oneself—be it as an "enemy of the people" or as a "little soldier for Mao."

It is not difficult to see that *fanshen* is experienced as most profoundly disturbing on the level of identity. Not only is the world redefined, with others reclassified, but the individual literally no longer knows who he is. At this point, all of reality becomes uncertain and threatened with meaninglessness—precisely the condition that sociologists commonly call anomie. Lukamba, an African interviewed by an ethnologist in the former Belgian Congo,[13] begins his autobiographical account in these words:

I was one of the last real people to be born to my tribe. I was born in a world that was not good, and was not bad, but it was more good than bad. There were other tribes around us that wanted to kill us because they wanted our land, but that was only because there were still others who wanted their land. We were powerful, and nobody conquered us, and we lived on between the two great rivers. Then the white man came and stopped all the fighting, and this was a good thing.

It is much less clear whether what happened later to Lukamba can also be described as a good thing. He went to a Christian mission school and subsequently worked for the white man. In the course of these changes he simultaneously realized the wealth of his traditional inheritance and the manner in which it was about to disappear:

I learned to feel close to the ancestors, and to know that we were one with them, although I still did not know where they lived or how. But when I put on the skin of the leopard and painted my body and became as a leopard, the ancestors talked to me, and I felt them all around me, I was never frightened at such times, but felt good. This is what we have lost, what we have had taken away from us. Now it is forbidden for us to talk to our ancestors, the Anyota is no more so we can no longer learn their will or call on them for help. We no longer have any reason for living, because we have been forced away from the ways of our ancestors, and we lead other men's lives, not the lives of our fathers.

The time span in which transformations of consciousness brought about by these collisions take place differ in different cases. In some the transformation is rapid or even cataclysmic. In others the transformation takes longer. The point is often argued (especially by analysts who are inimical to revolutionary change) that slower change is somehow "healthier." We do not think that such a concept has any place in a scientific analysis of these processes. It is essentially a value judgment. However, we would tend toward the hypothesis that there is an inverse relationship between the duration of such transformations and the degree of coercion necessary to bring them about.

The carry-over process from the primary carriers of modernization to other areas of social life also varies in effectiveness. While in most cases that are available to us it has been powerful and broadly successful, it would be a mistake to view such a process as irresistible or uniform in character. There is always the possibility that even when a primary carrier intrudes into a traditional situation, its modernizing effects will be contained within a highly specific, limited sector of social life for a considerable period of time. In other words, modernization may be *encapsulated,* contained in a kind of enclave, around which the traditional patterns of life go on substantially as before. An instructive case in point is provided by Manning Nash's study of the introduction of a modern factory into a Guatemalan village.[14] Nash analyzes in considerable detail the manner in which, within the setting of the factory, traditional patterns of life were transformed. His term for this, "factory rationality," refers to many of the processes discussed in the first chapter of this book. But Nash also shows how traditional categories of village life were prevented from being effective within the social experience of the factory. These traditional patterns were, so to speak, checked in at the factory gate. Outside that gate the life of the village went on in much the same way as it had. In Nash's example, a number of factors led to encapsulation, the principal one being that the factory in question, a textile plant, was technologically quite unsophisticated and therefore did not require very much training for local labor.

Encapsulation can be viewed as one pole in a continuum of carry-over intensities. At the other end is *fanshen*, in which carry-over is total, rapid and catastrophic. Between these two poles, there is a great variety of both carry-over and stoppage processes. We would contend that one of the main areas of research in the frame of reference we are presenting here should be the empirical investigation of the interplay of carry-over and stoppage in particular modernizing situations.

Between the two poles there are numerous possibilities of what might be called *cognitive bargaining*, that is, of compromises on the levels of consciousness between traditional and modern patterns. R. S. Khare's study of a Hindu caste association provides an interesting case study of such compromises.[15] It is hard to imagine a more massively traditional social structure than the Indian caste system. Modern India, however, has seen the development of caste associations, one of whose major purposes is to mediate between the traditional patterns of caste and the social realities of modernizing India. Many of the incidents Khare discusses are excellent illustrations of cognitive bargaining. For example, the father of a young man who had just taken a university degree used the "strategic connections" of his caste position to help his son obtain a government job.[16] Here, on the surface at least, the traditional network of personal relations directly collided with the impersonal merit system of a modern bureaucracy. Interestingly, the father's efforts on behalf of his son at no point specifically challenged the impersonal criteria of merit and fairness institutionalized in Indian government bureaucracy. Yet the traditional channels of communication and influence were skillfully brought into play "around" the modern structures with, in this particular case, formidable success. As the father succinctly summarized it: "I think it was both my son's good academic credentials and a helpful attitude of the caste elite. The latter was not spontaneously produced, it came out of the right approach and appropriate contacts."[17]

The compromises are likely to be most difficult and painful in the area of religion. One of the most general characteristics of traditional pre-modern societies is their symbolic integration by means of religion. This integration is in most cases critically challenged by the onset of modernization. At the conclusion of Chapter 3 we discussed the relationship of modernity to pluralism and secularization. We would maintain that the crisis of plausibility that religion has been going through in the Western world is intimately related to these features of modernity. In the Third World today the same developments are experienced as coming from without, that is, from the West. In the formerly colonial countries they have been coupled with frequently aggressive intervention by foreign political powers. This does not necessarily mean (and usually did not mean) that the colonial power deliberately wished to undermine the religious beliefs of the indigenous population. On the contrary, most Western colonial regimes were highly solicitous of traditional religion, partly, no doubt, because they considered it to be a pacifying force. Nevertheless, the exercise of political power by a Western government inevitably led to a shrinkage in the social influence of traditional religion. This effect is most visible in the area of law. Colonial regimes tended to arrogate to themselves at least the more serious sectors of criminal law, even if other legal matters were left to traditional authorities. In societies in which traditionally the entire body of law was under religious jurisdiction (as in the Islamic world) this arrogation was in itself a secularizing event. It followed logically that those sectors of law that came under direct colonial jurisdiction would be organized in terms of modern legal canons, which were usually, of course, derived from the colonial government's country of origin. Law became a secularizing agency directly sanctioned by political coercion. Postcolonial independent governments have very largely continued this level of secularization. Whether by design or default, there has therefore been a repetition in the Third World of the "solution" of the problem of religion in a pluralistic society—that is, privatization.

A general formula has been for the law to permit religious jurisdiction to continue over private matters, especially those that concern the family, such as marriage, divorce, inheritance or the status of children. Outside of this private sector, however, in the area of the public institutions of the polity and the economy, the law has become increasingly secularized. A good illustration of this compromise is the passionate debate that took place after the establishment of Pakistan concerning the limits of traditional Muslim jurisdiction in the area of family law.[18] Generally speaking, the modernizing view on these matters has won the day. But this did not happen without fierce opposition from traditionalist sources. One major traditionalist argument, in Pakistan as elsewhere, has been that once traditional religious jurisdiction begins to be eroded it becomes increasingly difficult to arrest the process. One may say that the traditionalists have been quite correct sociologically in this apprehension.

The crisis of traditional religion in the Third World reveals, perhaps more sharply than anything else, the essential ordeal of modernization, the collective and individual loss of integrative meanings. For this reason, a yearning for reintegration is one of the most powerful realities of modernizing societies. This yearning may take the form of nostalgia for the integrative symbols of the past. It may also take the form of hope for a new integration to be achieved in some future redemption.

Ideologies: Modernization and Counter-Modernization

In the preceding two chapters we have looked at various cognitive responses to modernization on the level of everyday life. Let us turn now to another cognitive level, the level of deliberate and systematic reflection, or, to put it most simply, ideology. The term "ideology" has had a number of different meanings in the social sciences. We use it here in a very broad sense, as referring to any theoretically articulated propositions about social reality. There are three different types of ideological response to modernization. First, there are ideologies that directly endorse or legitimate modernization. Next, there are ideologies developed in opposition or resistance to modernization; these might be called counter-modernization ideologies. Third, and most important of all today, there are ideologies that seek to control or contain modernization in the name of values that are conceived to be independent of that process.

Again, we think it is useful to approach the topic by first looking at polar opposites. At one pole we find an idea of modernization as redemption. At the other pole we find the idea that modernization is tantamount to damnation. At the first pole, ideology legitimates the attachment of profound hope and aspiration to the modernizing process. At the other pole, the modernizing process is ideologically represented as a dehumanizing oppression that must be resisted at all cost. As we previously saw with collisions of consciousness on the level of everyday life, there is a variety of intermediate positions between the poles. And we should not be surprised that in the Third World today it is the intermediate positions that are of greatest importance.

Although it is probably not a pure case, the so-called Cargo Cult is an instructive example of modernization being legitimated in redemptive terms.[1] The ideology in this case is clearly religious. The Cargo Cult flourished in different parts of Melanesia during the early decades of this century. Its core was a prophecy. White men would arrive on ships (in more recent versions, planes have taken the place of ships). These white men were the dead returned from the other world. Upon arrival they would distribute goods to all the people, and everyone would be very happy as a result. These goods (that is, the ships' cargo, from which the movement derived its name) were invariably modern industrial consumer goods, which became charged with redemptive significance. The case is not pure because it contains the elements of traditionalism that have led to the classification of the Cargo Cult under the ethnological category of "nativism," a category that usually refers to counter-modernizing rather than modernizing movements and ideas. While there may well be such elements in the Cargo Cult (the identification of the cargo-bearing white men with the dead is a case in point), we think this particular movement is profoundly illustrative of one pole of ideological responses.

Redemptive hopes and expectations are here linked to precisely those gifts of modernity that are brought by the West on its ships and planes. Happiness consists in the acquisition of as many of these goods as is possible. If we take *this* to be the key motif of the Cargo Cult, then it represents a very widespread ideological response indeed. We could even say that *all* ideologies that directly legitimate modernization are quite literally "cargo cults," such as the vision of the Turkish grocer mentioned in the preceding chapter. On the level of more sophisticated theory, this generalized "cargo cult" is what Marxist critics in Latin America have (pejoratively) called *desarrollismo*.[2] The term literally means developmentalism. It refers to all theories and ideologies that regard development in the sense of economic growth and institutional modernization as a good in itself. "Developmentalism" in this sense has, until very recently, been the underlying assumption of most North American social scientists dealing with Third World problems. Whether or not one agrees with the other positions of the Marxist critics, one is indebted to them for pointing out, very correctly, that developmentalism is not a necessary and value-free scientific position, but rather is based upon an implicit ideology. This ideology is, however, by no means limited to the United States. With considerable differences in detail, the official Soviet notions of development could also be quite aptly subsumed under the same general ideological category.[3] Unlike their American counterparts, Soviet developmental theorists have, of course, emphasized the importance of a revolutionary restructuring of traditional societies before the redemptive benefits of modernity can be fully savored. We would not minimize the importance of this difference. What remains quite similar is the uncritical legitimation of modernity in opposition to all traditional ways of life. One need mention only the Soviet glorification of such things as rural electrification or the mechanization of agriculture, not merely in their own country, but in any part of the Third World into which Soviet development programs have been extended. Only recently a Soviet official proudly stated on American television, "Our aim is the full automobilization of Soviet society." To the extent that Soviet society is upheld as the great model for the Third World to follow, this attitude represents a "cargo cult" in pretty clear form.

At the opposite pole, there are various forms of counter-modernizing ideology. These generally include what is commonly called nativism.[4] The distinguishing characteristic here is a defensive reaffirmation of traditional symbols. A convenient case to compare with the aforementioned Melanesian movement is the Ghost Dance of the Prairie Indians between 1870 and 1890.[5] Here, too, there was a prophecy proclaiming the imminent return of the dead. Unlike the Melanesian dead, however, the returned Indians would chase away the whites and restore the traditional way of life. The whole world of modern America would disappear like a bad dream and the Indians would return to the allegedly happy days of the past. The practical consequence of the Ghost Dance for its followers was a radical rejection of all accommodations to the white culture. Adherents had to lead a rigorously traditional life, and any deviation was considered treason to the movement.

The Ghost Dance was, in the main, a peaceful affair,

though its symbols linked its adherents to earlier movements of armed resistance against the whites. (Also, presumably, there was to be a good deal of violence when the prophecy reached fulfillment.) Nativism frequently takes a violent form, however. A classical case was the Japanese elimination of all Western influences in the seventeenth century. Here, a deliberate attempt was made to wipe out every vestige of Western influence and, indeed, everyone, either native or foreign, who had in any way become contaminated by modern importations. The attempt was successful to an amazing degree; it kept Japan rigorously isolated from modernizing influences until the Meiji Restoration of a little over a century ago. A more recent example of such violent counter-modernization is the Mahdi rebellion in the Sudan.[6] Here counter-modernization was legitimated ideologically in explicitly religious terms. The rebellion was led by a man who claimed to be the Mahdi, that is, the savior foretold in Muslim tradition who would establish the universal empire of Islam. The rebels, against the British and their Egyptian allies, were engaged in a *jihad*, a holy war as commanded by the Islamic faith. Such a war is fought in defense of everything that is traditionally regarded as sacred and humanly worthwhile. Opposition to modernity was total. Modernity became a malignant monster that must be eradicated in fire and blood. The religious context provided an ultimate legitimation of the impulse of resistance and rebellion.

In the contemporary Third World, nativism in one modification or another continues in various traditionalist ideologies that seek to maintain or (more commonly) to revitalize an indigenous tradition in the face of modernization. On the level of pretheoretical or nontheoretical consciousness (the level of the "man in the street") counter-

modernization still quite frequently takes the form of pure
and total opposition to modernity. Such absolute traditionalism is, however, becoming rare on the level of systematic ideology. More commonly, what one finds is one
notion or another of seeking *control* over the forces of
modernization in the name of traditional symbols. Most
ideological responses to modernization today, even if they
take a traditionalist coloration, are ideologies of control
rather than ideologies of outright opposition. In other
words, there is a general effort to synthesize, both in
theory and in practice, the impulses of modernization and
counter-modernization.

While we may thus still find traditionalism (we prefer this term to nativism) in various parts of the Third
World, it is rarely expressed as direct opposition to modernity. Rather, there is the ambition to combine development and modernization with the protection of traditional
symbols and patterns of life. Very importantly, this desire
for continuity with indigenous traditions focuses on the
public as well as the private spheres of social life. The
traditionalist is typically not satisfied with the relega-
tion of traditional ways to the private sphere. The
public sphere as well, particularly its political and legal
institutions, must retain allegiance to the traditional
symbols.

Mahatma Gandhi was probably the most important
traditionalist thinker of the twentieth century. A basic impulse of the Gandhian movement was to resist modernization in all spheres of life and (albeit with important modifications, as for instance with regard to the caste system)
to achieve the independence of India in accordance with
traditional Hindu ideas. While the importance of Gandhian thought for the political reality of India has greatly
diminished since independence, there continue to be important movements that express the Gandhian point of

view. One of these is the Vinoba Bhave.[7] The major aim of this movement is to bring about land reform by persuading landlords to surrender land voluntarily to the poor. Beyond this pragmatic goal, however, is the continuing Gandhian ambition to revitalize Indian society by ideas and values derived from the tradition of Hinduism. The Gandhian ideology shows very clearly one widespread characteristic in contemporary forms of traditionalism: while tradition is defended, it is at the same time greatly modified. Thus while Gandhi was inimical to industrialization and to many other aspects of the modern world as brought to India by the British, he was given to a religious syncretism that would be abhorrent to a fully traditional Hindu. He was willing to accept the modern concepts of the nation-state and of political democracy for independent India, and (probably most important of all in the Hindu context) he was in favor of radical modifications of the caste system, to the point of abolishing the lowest categories in that system.

This characteristic of most traditionalist ideologies replicates on the theoretical level what we previously called cognitive bargaining on the level of everyday consciousness. Behind this phenomenon lies a simple but profoundly important mechanism of human cognition: *Almost any contact between different cognitive systems leads to mutual contamination.*[8] The traditionalist defending himself cognitively against modernity almost inevitably incorporates elements of the latter within his own defense. This process of cognitive contamination operates mainly in one direction because modernity is represented in the traditionalist's milieu by overwhelmingly powerful political and economic agents. Thus it is the traditionalist, rather than the modernizer, who experiences the greatest pressures toward compromise in his ideological constructions.

Rich material on the continuing importance of traditionalism (in terms of both movements and ideologies) can be found in the contemporary Muslim world.[9] There is the extremely instructive case of the attempt to construct a state in Pakistan that would be both explicitly Muslim and explicitly modern. There is the more recent case of the resurgence of militant Islamic traditionalism in the revolutionary regimes in Algeria and in Libya. In the three cases just mentioned, and in others, there is the common feature of attempting to combine a resurgent Islam with a commitment to such modern goals as economic development, social progress and political democracy. Beyond this, however, there is the desire to show that the traditional culture (in this case Muslim) is actually *conducive* to these modern goals.

In other Muslim countries, however, traditionalist movements have repeatedly been in conflict with regimes that have pursued the goals of modern development. The clash between the Nasserite regime in Egypt and the Muslim Brotherhood is an important case in point. There have been similar conflicts in other parts of the Muslim world, for example in Pakistan and in Indonesia. The recurring motif in these conflicts is the assertion by the more rigid traditionalists that the modernizing regimes have diluted or misused the traditional symbols. Such conflicts are not limited to the Muslim world. Similar constellations can be found in a number of countries where an attempt was made to harness Buddhist traditions to the processes of development and modernization, as in Burma, Thailand and Ceylon.[10] The recurring problem for traditionalists of all colorations is the problem of just where to draw the line—that is, the line beyond which compromises (in practice as well as in ideology) no longer maintain the tradition but serve to liquidate it from within. We doubt that there is any generally applicable formula to solve this problem, which means that it is likely to continue to haunt any efforts to synthesize modernization and counter-modernization under the banner of traditional symbols.

The most potent form of ideological response to modernization in the Third World today is nationalism.[11] There is considerable irony in this. Nationalism, indeed the very idea of nation and nation-state, is a peculiarly Western construction. In the Third World the same construction has become an anti-Western ideology. Furthermore, nationalism is a peculiarly modern ideology, a product of the same bourgeois class that created modern capitalism and modern democracy. At least as far back as the Napoleonic period, nationalism appeared on the political scene as a force claiming to represent progress and modernity. Yet, in the Third World, it has been nationalism that has repeatedly attempted to incorporate into itself the counter-modernizing impulses discussed above.

Nationalism depends upon a particular social definition of the situation, that is, upon a collectively agreed-upon entity known as a particular nation. While political scientists have tried to arrive at some intrinsic elements required for nationality (such as common territory, common history and the like), the definition of a particular group of people as constituting a nation is always an act of social construction of reality. That is, it is always "artificial." This is as much the case with France as with, say, Zambia. The difference between France and Zambia is not that the former is in some way less "artificial" a construction than the latter, but rather that the construction has been around for a longer time. People in France have had a better chance to habituate themselves to the self-identification of Frenchmen than Zambians have to their self-identification in terms of Zambia as a nation. In some parts of the Third World, nationalism has been able to attach itself to older political identities. This has been typically the case in areas where there are traditions of powerful political entities in the past, such as India or China. In such places nationalism can link up more readily with older traditions. In Africa, by contrast, where nations were newly defined within old colonial boundaries, the task of "nation building" (or, if one prefers, the task of *inventing* nations) has been much more difficult.[12]

In either type of situation, nationalism entails the construction of new overarching symbols. The avowed purpose of the construction is, typically, first the mobilization of people to obtain independence from foreign rule or domination, and second, mobilization to attain the goals of development policies. The nation is defined as an all-embracing community, and thus is posited as an entity that can overcome the fragmentations and alienations of the modernizing process. The nation provides a new collective identity and, at least to a degree, an identity for the individual as well.

The symbols of nationalism have been very effective indeed in situations where there has been a struggle for independence, either in the literal sense of throwing out a colonial regime or, more indirectly, in the sense of liberation from foreign domination or influence (in the recent history of Latin America it is the latter rather than the former aspiration that must be taken into account). In such situations, nationalism provides integrative symbolism for variegated groups within the society. Once the struggle had ended in success, however, the symbols of nationalism frequently lose their integrative potency. Other collective identifications and solidarities emerge, or re-emerge. African "tribalism" is perhaps the clearest case of this. Ethnic, linguistic or religious collectivities appear as challengers to the symbolic supremacy of the nation, and of the state that claims to embody it. In such situations, the nation state and its political institutions become the major modernizing symbol *against* the impulses of counter-modernization.

In the ideology of socialism in the Third World there are a number of issues that we cannot deal with here.[13] Most important, we cannot adjudicate the question as to whether socialism does or does not constitute the most viable model of development in terms of economic growth or collective happiness or, for that matter, social justice. To discuss the first two matters would transcend the scope of this book; to discuss the third would entail transcending the limits of social science. Yet there are a number of observations about socialism that must be made within our limited scope. We would emphasize once again that in our opinion these observations can be made quite independently of the way in which one answers (positively *or* negatively) the question about the general viability of the socialist model.

As we have indicated before, we think there is a hidden agenda to socialism in the Third World that is only indirectly related to the pragmatic economic, social and political issues that socialist ideology addresses itself to. This hidden agenda is the theme of community posited *against* the disintegrative forces of modernization. In this central motif, Third World socialism is very close indeed to Third World nationalism (despite the frequently quixotic efforts of United States foreign policy to make subtle distinctions between the two). However, the community that socialism posits is both more universal and more specific than the community defined by nationalism. It is more universal because most socialist ideologies make an appeal to a common human destiny that transcends the borders of the national society. It is more specific because it addresses itself not only to the various traditional differentiations of society (tribe, caste, religion and so on), but in addition, seeks to solve the problem of the *new* differentiations that modernization itself has brought about. These differentiations are very largely understood by socialist ideologies in terms of class. It is the community of the oppressed, the poor, the exploited, that is both defined and constructed by socialist movements.

As in the case of Third World nationalism, the most important carrier group of the ideology is the "intellectuals." The meaning of this term in the Third World is somewhat different from the meaning to which Westerners are accustomed. To be an "intellectual" means to have successfully completed a certain amount of education, sometimes no more than secondary school. Both socialism and nationalism are initially propagated by a relatively small stratum of such "intellectuals," employed in the lower reaches of the political, educational and economic institutions of the society. With the coming of independence, this stratum is supported to a very high degree by government employment. Socialism and nationalism, then, not only constitute ideological preferences of intellectuals, but become official doctrines, legitimated by government from the highest to the lowest echelons.

The merging of the nationalist and socialist ideological response to modernization is very explicit in many areas. Important cases are "Indian socialism," "Arab socialism," and "African socialism." In each one of these cases, there is not only a merger of the two ideologies, but the further assumption that the national genius in each particular case will necessitate or facilitate a peculiar *type* of socialism. Often it is a little difficult to determine in just what way this is supposed to be the case, but this indeterminacy in ideological content in no way detracts from the potency of the symbol, and quite possibly adds to it.

The coalescence of nationalism and socialism is of particular international relevance today in terms of the split between the Soviet and the Chinese versions of Communist internationalism.[14] The Soviet model of socialist development has been widely discredited because of the belief that it seeks to impose an alien (namely its own) system upon all societies that come under its domination. By contrast, the Chinese version of Communism, and the Maoist model of development, have represented themselves with considerable success in various parts of the Third World as an ideology that is highly respectful of indigenous traditions and particular local circumstances. The extent to which this image of Maoism may be an illusion need not concern us here.

Socialism in any of its versions represents itself as a *combination* of community and progress, of collective solidarity and development. While most versions of socialist ideology acknowledge that development and modernization entail sacrifices, there is a strong emphasis on such sacrifices being borne equitably and in fraternal solidarity by the society as a whole. To the extent that modernization has up to now entailed a fragmentation and disintegration of communal solidarities, socialism promises to reverse the trend. It offers modernity *and* community. Indeed, one may say that socialism, as an ideology, says quite literally that one can have one's cake and eat it too. Socialism in the Third World, of course, defines itself in opposition to a specific image of capitalism, which emphasizes its allegedly intrinsic exploitative and divisive characteristics. Socialist cooperation is posited against capitalist competition. Socialism is defined as a purveyor of collective identity, while capitalism is seen as bringing about the alienation and isolation of the individual. It hardly needs emphasizing that there are very strong redemptive undertones in all of this.

These themes are often linked explicitly to pre-modern indigenous patterns. A good example is Tanzania. In the so-called Arusha Declaration of 1967, TANU, the ruling party of Tanzania under the regime of Julius Nyerere, proclaimed the ideology of a distinctive African socialism as the guideline for the country's development. A key term in this ideology is *ujamaa*. This is a Swahili term which cannot be precisely translated but which refers to the indigenous African patterns of kinship or clan solidarity. TANU declared that *ujamaa* would be the basic norm for the development of Tanzanian society as a whole. The new socialism would link up directly and naturally with the indigenous African approach to social life. This is how Nyerere himself explains the concept:

Ujamaa, then, or "familyhood," describes our socialism. It is opposed to capitalism, which seeks to build a happy society on the basis of the exploitation of man by man; and it is equally opposed to doctrinaire socialism which seeks to build its happy society on a philosophy of inevitable conflict between man and man. We, in Africa, have no more need of being "converted" to socialism than we have of being "taught" democracy. Both are rooted in our own past—in the traditional society which produced us. Modern African socialism can draw from its traditional heritage the recognition of "society" as an extension of the basic family unit. But it can no longer confine the idea of the social family within the limits of the tribe, nor, indeed, of the nation. For no true African socialist can look at a line drawn on a map and say "the people on this side of that line are my brothers, but those who happen to live on the other side of it can have no claim on me"; every individual on this continent is his brother.[15]

Closely related to this in Tanzania is the notion of *controlled* development, in terms of indigenous values and indigenous resources. The country is to be fully in charge of its own development policies. It is to seek its own solutions to its problems of underdevelopment, and to reject the arbitrary imposition of models derived from abroad. In line with these ambitions, Tanzania has placed a major emphasis on rural and agrarian development, as against rapid industrialization. A growing network of so-called *ujamaa* villages (collective agricultural settlements planned by the government) is to provide a sound base for the modernization of agriculture while at the same time preventing the dislocations and conflicts that have gone with modernization elsewhere. There has also been a policy of encouraging people to remain on the land to forestall the chaotic growth of cities so typical of the Third World.

We cannot discuss here the extent to which these particular policies have been successful in Tanzania. But the thinking underlying the Tanzanian model of African socialism is by no means limited to that country. It represents a spreading conviction in the Third World (in Asia and Latin America as well as in Africa) that these societies will have to design their own conceptions of development and to base their development planning on self-reliance rather than on dependence on foreign assistance. In line with this, a slogan has gained currency in recent years among Third World intellectuals: "Development without modernization." The meaning is quite simple: it endorses the goals of development in the sense of economic growth and an equitable distribution of its benefits, in terms of better health, better housing, better education and so forth. At the same time, it rejects the notion that these development goals necessitate the modernization of the entire society in the sense of adopting Western-derived institutions. Both development and modernization are to be subject to controls based on deliberately chosen values in each country.

Notions such as these bring us to the last ideological response that we would like to discuss here—one that for lack of a better term we call post-modernism. This is a response that bears considerable similarity to demodernizing impulses in the advanced industrial societies themselves (which we will take up in the following chapters). The root idea is, again, quite simple: modernity has run its course, modernization and development must be fundamentally challenged as goals for the Third World, and quite new approaches to the human problems of poverty and injustice must be invented. In other words: the Turkish grocer should have second thoughts about his vision.

The ideas of Ivan Illich, which have gained some attention in Latin America, may be taken as representative of this novel ideological response.[16] A few years ago Illich began to analyze the school as an institution imposed by the modern world on Latin America. He tried to show in a number of sharply critical analyses that the school in Latin America was inimical to the avowed purpose of development and also to profoundly important human values. The school served to legitimate social inequalities by using educational achievement in its own terms as a criterion for social stratification. The school indoctrinated people in values destructive of traditional solidarity and conducive to capitalist exploitation. Illich called for a fundamental rethinking of the conception of education, which he felt would lead to a "cultural revolution" in other areas of social life as well.

At least in his own work this has been the case. In the recent past, Illich has turned from the school to other institutions linked to modernization and subjected them to equally sharp critiques. He has dealt with modern systems of public health, transportation and housing, in each case trying to show that these institutions, as they are currently developing in Latin America, enslave rather than liberate man. The post-modern utopia that Illich suggests, which he calls a "convivial society," would be characterized above all by a rejection of the modern ideas of unending growth, unilinear progress and ever more expansive rationality. At the same time, this utopia is not antitechnological. On the contrary, it would use the most sophisticated techniques available in contemporary society to permit the creation of new, deliberately planned human communities. Inevitably, the emphasis would be on communities of limited size, with both modern technology and the mechanisms of political decision accessible to everyone.

Illich's term, "cultural revolution" (a rather unfortunate choice, since Illich in no way regards Communist China as a model for his thinking) suggests that a fundamental transformation must take place on the level of consciousness. In other words, what he proposes are new and revolutionary theoretical approaches to the problems of the Third World. In this he is close to the ideas of the Brazilian educator Paulo Freire, who developed a method of education he called "conscientization."[17] Originally the term, as used by Freire, simply meant that adults could be taught anything more readily if the teaching was related to the primary concerns of their everyday life.

(Freire was originally concerned with teaching literacy.) The term, however, has come to mean much more than that, both in Freire's own work and in its wide diffusion among radical intellectuals throughout Latin America. Conscientization now means the entire transformation of the consciousness of people that would make them understand the political parameters of their existence and the possibilities of changing their situation by political action. Conscientization is a precondition of liberation. People will be able to liberate themselves from social and political oppression only if they first liberate themselves from the patterns of thought imposed by the oppressors. In Latin America these ideas have become particularly powerful in the Catholic left and have become incorporated in a body of thought generally known as "the theology of liberation."[18] One aspect of this ideology, which we cannot pursue here, is the legitimation of revolutionary aspirations by Christian theology. This has become politically important in recent years in a number of Latin American countries, spectacularly so in Chile. More germane to our present considerations, however, is the nature of the "liberation" being proclaimed. It could be aptly described as a liberation *beyond* modernity. It envisages a new type of society, which would be neither a return to the traditional structures, nor an approximation of contemporary advanced industrial societies. Most exponents of this ideology envisage an economy run along socialist lines, but (even if Marxism is often accepted as a valid method of analysis) there is the general tendency to reject all existing socialist societies as models and to envisage a future socialism that does not as yet exist.

There is an underlying paradox in all ideologies that seek to control or contain modernity, a paradox closely related to the phenomenon that we have called cognitive contamination: if one wishes to control modernization, one must assume one has an option and the ability to manipulate. Thus one may opt against modernity. Thus one will seek to manipulate the processes of modernization. These very ideas, however, are modern—indeed, modernizing—*in themselves*. Nothing could be more modern than the idea that man has a choice between different paths of social development. One of the most pervasive characteristics of traditional societies is the notion that there is no choice; that the structures of the given society are inevitable, rooted in human nature, or indeed in the very constitution of the cosmos. Similarly, the notion that the course of human events can be deliberately manipulated and controlled is a specifically modern notion, which is alien to the thinking of most people in traditional societies. Therefore, at least in this one fundamental theme, modern consciousness is a well-nigh irresistible force, and it imposes the theme of option and manipulability even on those who most strenuously resist it.

A number of general questions express the underlying problem to which all of the aforementioned ideologies address themselves: Is the process of modernization, as hitherto experienced, irrevocable and irresistible? Are there alternatives to it? In our own terms, what are the possibilities of stoppage?

All these questions are, of course, susceptible to being answered in terms of the available Western "solution" of the dichotomization between public and private spheres. It would be possible to concede the irrevocability and irresistibility of modernization in the institutions of the public sphere and to look upon the private sphere as a refuge or "reservation" for other structures of consciousness and patterns of life. None of the aforementioned ideologies, however, are willing to settle for this. Indeed, the dichotomization is one of the allegedly dehumanizing aspects of modernity *from which* liberation is sought. So one comes to a very specific question: What are the possibilities of stoppage *within* the public sphere? This question entails implications that are beyond our scope here. Some of these implications have to do with the economic feasibility, or the political requirements, of certain development models. However, it should be clear by now that the question also entails implications on the level of consciousness. Whatever might be the economic and political parameters necessary for the realization of development models that seek alternatives to what has hitherto been called modernity, there remains the question of the intrinsic linkage between certain institutional processes and certain structures of consciousness, and this underlies some of the most urgently discussed problems in the Third World today.

III

DEMODERNIZATION

And now what will become of us without Barbarians?—
Those people were some sort of a solution.

—C. P. CAVAFY

8

Modernity and Its Discontents

In the first part of this book we mentioned the discontents and counterformations engendered by the institutional structures of modernity. Let us summarize these and then discuss the institutional dynamics within which they are located.

First there are discontents that derive directly or indirectly from the technologized economy. Most generally, these are the discontents derived from what Max Weber called "rationalization." The rationality that is intrinsic to modern technology imposes itself upon both the activity and the consciousness of the individual as control, limitation and, by the same token, frustration. Irrational impulses of all sorts are progressively subjected to controls. (The Freudian term "repression" is singularly apt for describing this process.) The result is considerable psychological tension. The individual is forced to "manage" his emotional life, transferring to it the engineering ethos of modern technology. The discontents derived from this source are broader in scope, however. As we have seen, modern technological production brings about an anonymity in the area of social relations. What we have called componentiality, which is intrinsically related to the manner in which modern technology deals with material objects, is transferred to individual relations with others, and ultimately with the self. This anonymity carries with it a constant threat of anomie. The individual is threatened not only by meaninglessness in the world of his work, but also by the loss of meaning in wide sectors of his relations with other people. The very complexity and pervasiveness of the technologized economy makes more and more social relations opaque to the individual. The institutional fabric as a whole tends toward incomprehensibility. Even in the individual's everyday experience, other individuals appear as agents of forces and collectivities which he does not understand. Furthermore, he is constantly in the situation of having too many balls in the air simultaneously. In the words of the classical American joke: He has "too many choices" all the time. The complexity of the multi-relational modern world puts a strain on all standard operating procedures, not only in the individual's activity but in his consciousness as well. The typologies and interpretive schemes by which everyday life is ordered (and thus becomes possible as the arena of social interaction) must be used from moment to moment to deal with vastly complicated and constantly changing demands. Once more the result is tension, frustration and, in the extreme case, a feeling of being alienated from others.

The discontents derived from the bureaucratization

of major institutions are very similar to the ones just mentioned. However, they are even broader in scope for the simple reason that bureaucratization has affected nearly every sector of social life. To be sure, the goods and services provided by the technologized economy also pervade everyday life. But many of them can be incorporated into various social contexts without immediately changing their character. A congregation of Tibetan Buddhist monks, let us say, transplanted to the United States, can start using electric razors without thereby altering the character of their social relations. If, however, this monastic community started to bureaucratize its procedures, the very fabric of its social life would change almost immediately. The individual is "surrounded" by bureaucracy far more effectively than he is by the technologized economy, at least as far as his social life is concerned. Therefore, while the discontents of bureaucracy are similar to those brought about by the technologized economy, the individual is more likely to suffer from the former than from the latter.

The primary and most powerful location of bureaucracy is in the political sphere, and it is here that these discontents have had their most spectacular expression. Increasingly in advanced industrial societies (apparently regardless of their particular ideological or institutional character), people have come to feel "alienated" from the polity and its symbols. Political life has become anonymous, incomprehensible and anomic to broad strata of the population. However, it would be a mistake to limit one's understanding of the discontents of bureaucracy to the political area. It is much more pervasive than that. *All* the major public institutions of modern society have become "abstract."[1] That is, these institutions are experienced as formal and remote entities with little or no meaning that can be concretized in the living experience of the individual.

There are also discontents specifically derived from the pluralization of social life-worlds. Generally, these discontents can be subsumed under the heading of "homelessness." The pluralistic structures of modern society have made the life of more and more individuals migratory, ever-changing, mobile. In everyday life the modern individual continuously alternates between highly discrepant and often contradictory social contexts. In terms of his biography, the individual migrates through a succession of widely divergent social worlds. Not only are an increasing number of individuals in a modern society uprooted from their original social milieu, but, in addition, no succeeding milieu succeeds in becoming truly "home" either. It is important to understand, as we tried to show earlier, that this external mobility has correlates on the level of consciousness. A world in which everything is in constant motion is a world in which certainties of any kind are hard to come by. Social mobility has its correlate in cognitive and normative mobility. What is truth in one context of the individual's social life may be error in another. What was considered right at one stage of the individual's social career becomes wrong in the next. Once more, the anomic threat of these constellations is very powerful indeed.

The "homelessness" of modern social life has found its most devastating expression in the area of religion. The general uncertainty, both cognitive and normative, brought about by the pluralization of everyday life and of biography in modern society, has brought religion into a serious crisis of plausibility. The age-old function of religion—to provide ultimate certainty amid the exigencies of the human condition—has been severely shaken. Because of the religious crisis in modern society, social "homelessness" has become metaphysical—that is, it has become "homelessness" in the cosmos. This is very difficult to bear. The problem becomes most clearly apparent when one looks at that ancient function of religion which Weber called "theodicy." This means any explanation of human events that bestows meaning upon the experiences of suffering and evil. Through most of human history, religion provided such theodicies. In one way or another, religion made meaningful even the most painful experiences of the human condition, whether caused by natural or by social agents. Modern society has threatened the plausibility of religious theodicies, but it has not removed the experiences that call for them. Human beings continue to be stricken by sickness and death; they continue to experience social injustice and deprivation. The various secular creeds and ideologies that have arisen in the modern era have been singularly unsuccessful in providing satisfactory theodicies. It is important to understand the additional burden to modernity implicit in this. Modernity has accomplished many far-reaching transformations, but it has not fundamentally changed the finitude, fragility and mortality of the human condition. What it has accomplished is to seriously weaken those definitions of reality that previously made that human condition easier to bear. This has produced an anguish all its own, and one that we are inclined to think adds additional urgency and weight to the other discontents we have mentioned.

Modern society's "solution" to these discontents has been, as we have seen, the creation of the private sphere as a distinctive and largely segregated sector of social life, along with the dichotomization of the individual's societal involvements between the private and the public spheres. The private sphere has served as a kind of balancing mechanism providing meanings and meaningful activities to compensate for the discontents brought about by the large structures of modern society. In the private sphere, "repressed" irrational impulses are allowed to come to the fore. A specific private identity provides shelter from the threats of anonymity. The transparency of the private world makes the opacity of the public one tolerable. A limited number of highly significant relationships, most of them chosen voluntarily by the individual, provide the emotional resources for coping with the multi-relational reality "outside." Even religion has become largely privatized, with its plausibility structure shifting from society as a whole to much smaller groups of confirmatory individuals.[2]

There can be no doubt that this "solution" has worked for many people. It has, however, a number of built-in weaknesses, all of them directly related to the location of the private sphere in society and to the structural characteristics that are the consequence of this location. One way of describing it is to say that the private sphere is "underinstitutionalized."[3] This means that the private sphere has a shortage of institutions that firmly and reliably structure human activity. There are, of course, institutions within the private sphere. The most important of these is the family, which still derives legitimation and legal sanction from the state. There are also religious institutions, in whatever stage of privatization. There are voluntary associations, ranging from neighborhood improvement groups to hobby clubs. But none of these is in a position to organize the private sphere as a whole. The individual is given enormous latitude in fabricating his own particular private life—a kind of "do-it-yourself" universe.

This latitude obviously has its satisfactions, but it also imposes severe burdens. The most obvious is that most individuals *do not know how* to construct a universe and therefore become furiously frustrated when they are faced with a need to do so. The most fundamental function of institutions is probably to protect the individual from having to make too many choices. The private sphere has arisen as an interstitial area left over by the large institutions of modern society. As such, it has become under-institutionalized and therefore become an area of unparalleled liberty and anxiety for the individual. Whatever compensations the private sphere provides are usually experienced as fragile, possibly artificial and essentially unreliable.

Social life abhors a vacuum, probably for profound anthropological reasons. Human beings are not capable of tolerating the continuous uncertainty (or, if you will, freedom) of existing without institutional supports. Thus the underinstitutionalization of the private sphere has produced new institutional formations. These have been called "secondary institutions."[4] Some of them are old institutions that have been given new functions (such as the family or the church). Others are new institutions (such as the great variety of voluntary associations). They are meant to fill the gap left by the underinstitutionalization of the private sphere. There is, however, a built-in paradox in the way in which they function. If they retain the optional, and therefore artificial, quality of private life, they are not able to meet the demand for stability and reliability that brought them about in the first place. If, on the other hand, they are so constructed as to meet these demands, they increasingly take on the character of the larger institutions of modern society: they become bureaucratized, and therefore anonymous, abstract, anomic. As a result of its built-in weaknesses and the very largely built-in difficulties of finding any institutional remedies, the private sphere's compensatory quality is constantly in peril. The discontents engendered by the structures of modernity in the public sphere have a disconcerting way of reappearing in the private sphere. In their private lives individuals keep on constructing and reconstructing refuges that they experience as "home." But, over and over again, the cold winds of "homelessness" threaten these fragile constructions. It would be an overstatement to say that the "solution" of the private sphere is a failure; there are too many individual successes. But it is always very precarious.

These discontents and the counterformations to which they have led have been present from the beginning of the modern era. Resistance to modernity and counter-modernizing movements and ideologies have been recurring phenomena in the Western history of the last two or three centuries. Some of them have been quite similar to corresponding phenomena in the contemporary Third World. The counterformations have been both "reactionary" and "revolutionary," depending on whether the resolution of the discontents has been sought in the past or the future. A pervasive and seemingly permanent theme has been opposition to the public/private dichotomy of modern life, and various ideologies and movements have derived their motivating force from the promise to bridge public and private spheres in either an old or a new solidarity. The major institutional candidate for this solidarity has been the modern state. This is not the place to expound on the profound irony of this in view of the intensely bureaucratic character of the state. The final irony has been totalitarianism in the twentieth century. In both its "right" and "left" expressions, contemporary totalitarianism has combined the most grandiose promises of redemption from the discontents of modernity with the most extreme institutionalization of these same discontents.

Counter-modernization merges into demodernization at whatever point one regards as the definitive establishment of modern society. The impulse to resist the new evils with which one is beset then becomes a quest for liberation from the evils that one has already experienced. In the contemporary world we find a strange constellation of processes: modernization continues to go on throughout the world, not only in the underdeveloped countries but within various "pockets" of the advanced industrial societies themselves;[5] counter-modernization continues to be an important impulse in the Third World; and there has been an astonishingly powerful resurgence of demodernization in the most developed societies. Modernization, counter-modernization and demodernization must, therefore, be seen as *concurrent processes*.

An interesting historical question, which we cannot possibly pursue here, is whether there was a certain point of "optimum balance" in the development of the modern West, a point at which counter-modernizing forces had declined while demodernizing ones had as yet barely made their appearance. Perhaps the most likely time to locate this point would be the nineteenth century in Western Europe and North America, the century that marked the triumph of the bourgeoisie (the modernizing class *par excellence*) as well as the most strongly legitimated plausibility of the so-called Protestant ethic. But whether or not there was such a point, this is certainly not the situation today. The discontents of modernity are growing in advanced industrial societies, the old "solutions" are losing plausibility, and there seems to be an increasing incidence of demodernizing ideas and movements. The last seems to be particularly the case in the very recent past, especially in America. While there can be no certainty about the reasons for this, a number of them can be surmised.

One basic reason is undoubtedly the sheer intensification and acceleration of technological and bureaucratic processes. Modern scientific and technological advances have accelerated enormously in recent years and continue to accelerate, presumably as a result of their intrinsic logic and operation. There is no corresponding intrinsic accelerating factor in bureaucracy. Its growth has rather been the consequence of the increasing complexity of the world created by modern technology and the enormous increase in population which require even larger and ever more refined administrative structures. Quite simply, then, the primary carriers of modernity have become ever more powerful. Concurrently, the discontents produced by these primary carriers have increased in intensity and have stimulated the upsurge of strong demodernizing impulses.

There has been a concomitant development of the secondary carriers, particularly urbanization, both in the literal sense of the growth of cities and in the extended sense of the diffusion of urban ways of life. Thus there has also been an intensification and acceleration of the pluralization of all aspects of social life, bringing with it a deepening of those discontents that are primarily traceable to pluralization. Among these we would once more emphasize the deepening religious crisis.

One qualitative, rather than quantitative, change brought about by technological advances has been the economic shift from production to consumption. The advanced industrial societies today are characterized economically by the enormous growth of the so-called tertiary sector—that is, that sector of economic activity not directly related either to agriculture or to the production of industrial goods. This change has been so major that a number of analysts have suggested that contemporary society in Western Europe and North America be called "post-industrial."[6] While we are not enthusiastic about this term, there is no question that it refers to a very real and very important development. The consequences of this shift in the character of the economy for everyday life has been the growth not only of affluence but also of leisure. Less and less time is spent by most individuals in the world of productive labor of any kind. Concomitantly, more and more time is spent in private life. This shift in the "time budgets" of most people has put additional strain upon the private sphere and on its "solutions" to the problem of modern discontents. The search for satisfactory meanings for individual and collective existence has become, in consequence, more frantic.

There is an additional causal factor for the recent intensification of demodernizing impulses. This factor, though rarely noted, is, in our opinion, of very great importance indeed. It is rooted in the peculiarly modern transformation in the biographical stages of childhood and youth.[7]

The modern bourgeoisie produced a new world of childhood. The structural precondition of this was the separation of the family from productive economic activity that resulted from capitalism and, more importantly, from the industrial revolution. With the firm establishment of industrialism in modern economies, very few people continued to work in the same place in which they lived with their families. Thus the family became a protective enclave from the harsh realities of economic life. The same enclave, of course, provided the location for childhood. The bourgeoisie developed an ethos of childhood that placed very great importance on this stage of biography, a viewpoint that was particularly expressed in the educational aspirations of this class. But even more fundamentally, the new ethos of childhood was based on the assumption that childhood was a very peculiar, and peculiarly valuable, phase in the individual's life. Bourgeois childhood became sheltered, tender and even "sentimental."

These developments go back at least to the seventeenth century and cannot by themselves explain the recent upsurge of demodernizing impulses. There are, however, two more recent developments which must be seen in conjunction with them. First, there has been the rapid lengthening of the educational process, expressed not only in the legal provisions forbidding child labor and making ever-longer periods in school compulsory for everyone, but in the tendency of more and more occupations to demand very long educational preparation for admission. This has led to an expanding scope of the biographical stage of youth, from perhaps two or three years a hundred years ago to what is now at least a decade for most individuals. Youth has become a very important biographical stage between childhood and full maturity. The ethos of this new youth, however, is based on the ethos of childhood that preceded it biographically. To the extent that the bourgeois ethos of tenderness (what one might call the "gentle revolution") has been successfully institutionalized and has penetrated other classes beyond the bourgeoisie, youth has become charged with very high personal expectations. But its structural location in modern society almost guarantees that these expectations will be disappointed.

Another much more recent factor that must be taken into account is itself the result of a particular brand of technology, namely, modern medicine. This factor is the dramatic decline in infant mortality and morbidity in the very recent past. It is very difficult to overestimate this fact. It can be stated quite simply: it is only in this century, and in many parts of even the Western world only a matter of one or two generations, that the great majority of newborn children grow up to full maturity. *Until very recently in human history, most children died. Today most children live to grow up.* This means, first of all, that contemporary childhood is sheltered from anguish and fear in a completely new way. One need only look at such recent documents as nineteenth-century biographies or memoirs to grasp the significance of this. There is also, however, another consequence—for the most realistic reasons, parents today are free to invest expectations in their children from the moment of birth that would have been quite unrealistic before. This is not to suggest that modern parents love their children more than parents of earlier generations. But they are psychologically free to express this love much more openly than was the case before the modern revolution in childhood. Before, every expression of love was inhibited by the probability that the loved child was unlikely to survive; today, parental love can be expressed in the realistic expectation that it will not imminently turn to grief.

The relation of these new modern worlds of childhood and youth to the discontents of modernity can be quickly grasped by comparing some of the fundamental values involved. The "gentle revolution" has been conducive to the socialization of individuals used to being treated as uniquely valuable persons, accustomed to having their opinions respected by all significant persons around them, and generally unaccustomed to harshness, suffering or, for that matter, any kind of intense frustration. Without intending the adjective to be pejorative, we may say that individuals produced by these socialization processes tend to be peculiarly "soft." It is precisely these individuals who, at a later stage in their biographies, confront the anonymous, impersonal "abstract" structures of the modern technological and bureaucratic world. Their reaction, predictably, is one of rage. What might appear to people socialized under different conditions as perhaps mild irritation is experienced as intolerable oppression by these children of the "gentle revolution." Not surprisingly, then, it is youth today that has become one of the most important locales for demodernizing movements and ideologies. Equally unsurprisingly, these have been characterized by a virulent anti-bureaucratic and anti-technological animus.

The situation of youth in modern society has been elegantly described by a British sociologist as follows: "The adolescent was invented at the same time as the steam engine. The principal architect of the latter was Watt in 1765, of the former Rousseau in 1762. Having invented the adolescent, society has been faced with two major problems: how and where to accommodate him in the social structure, and how to make his behavior accord with the specifications."[8]

In view of the foregoing considerations, we may add that the specifications are almost impossible to meet. Contemporary youth has been in ongoing rebellion against them. To some extent the confrontation between youth and the "abstract" structures of modern society has been class-specific. That is, it has been most intense in those strata which, in America, are generally called the upper middle class, for the simple reason that it is in those strata that the new ethos of childhood and the resulting socialization patterns have been most developed. Some of these values, however, have spread throughout the society, even if different strata have had different reactions.

The individual passing through the stages of childhood

and youth lives a largely private life, even if it is "contained" by various educational institutions. Even the college student has as yet no "serious" stake in the publicly legitimated world, largely because of his peculiar relationship to productive activity (or rather, his *lack* of such relationship). This results in a curious situation: the private sphere, originally serving as a refuge from the discontents of modernity, now gives birth to violent reactions against the structures generating these discontents. Generally, attention has been focused on the campus as the primary locale of these rebellions. This, of course, is quite correct. We would suggest, however, that the events on the campus cannot be understood unless one sees them against the background of events in the nursery.[9]

The above considerations open to view a further paradox of great importance: modernity is understood by some as *liberating*, and by others as that *from which* liberation is sought. If one is to understand correctly the relation of various ideas and movements to the contemporary crisis of modern society, it is most important that one know *which* liberating aspiration is at work. It is also important to stress that as far as description goes, *both* liberation quests are valid. The final issue, of course, is not one of descriptive adequacy but a value judgment.

Modernity has indeed been liberating. It has liberated human beings from the narrow controls of family, clan, tribe or small community. It has opened up for the individual previously unheard-of options and avenues of mobility. It has provided enormous power, both in the control of nature and in the management of human affairs. However, these liberations have had a high price. Perhaps the easiest way to describe it is to refer to it once more as "homelessness." Demodernizing ideas and movements promise liberation from the many discontents of modernity. Again, the most economical way of describing the content of this promised liberation is to call it "home." The demodernizing impulse, whether it looks backward into the past or forward into the future, seeks a reversal of the modern trends that have left the individual "alienated" and beset with the threats of meaninglessness.[10]

The liberation of modernity has been, above all, that of the individual. Modern social structures have provided the context for the socialization of highly individuated persons. Concomitantly, modern society has given birth to ideologies and ethical systems of intense individualism. Indeed, it has been suggested that the theme of individual autonomy is perhaps the most important theme in the world view of modernity.[11] The experience of "alienation" is the symmetrical correlate of the same individuation. Put simply, "alienation" is the price of individuation. Quite logically, therefore, an important theme in demodernizing movements today is the protest against the allegedly excessive individualism of modern society. The individual is to be liberated *from* this individualism *to* the solidarity of either old or new collective structures.

In the advanced societies of the Western world the protest against individualism is specified in regard to capitalism and bourgeois democracy. Capitalism is perceived as a major fragmenting, "alienating" and ultimately dehumanizing force which pits individuals against each other in a merciless competitive conflict. Bourgeois democracy is understood as (in a Marxist sense) the "superstructure" of the capitalist system. The legal and political institutions of bourgeois democracy legitimate and perpetuate the dehumanizing individualism of capitalism. These perceptions, of course, reflect what may be called the "left mood" among contemporary intellectuals in

Western Europe and North America. It is important to see, however, that there are comparable phenomena on the "right." Conservative movements in advanced industrial societies (all the way back to Edmund Burke or, for that matter, Calhoun) have repeatedly contrasted the dehumanizing individualism of modernity with the safe and reliable collective security of pre-modern society. One of the underlying motifs of fascism (which one may call "right" or "left" with probably equal justification) was opposition to the individual egotism of bourgeois society and the proclamation of collective will and solidarity.

Nationalism, undoubtedly a product of the modern world, has been both a path toward and a reaction against universalism. In the Napoleonic ethos the nation was understood as a new community of liberated individuals and as a step toward the universal brotherhood of similarly liberated individuals throughout the world. Nationalism at this stage could clearly be understood as a modernizing force. Nationalism has, however, also become a reaction against such modern liberations, as a *return to* the containing and restrictive solidarities of collective life. Concomitantly, the nation-state has been perceived both as liberator and as oppressor. Thus, in the Third World today, nationalism appears as a predominantly modernizing force, liberating individuals and groups from the old controls of clan, tribe and the like. Nationalism in the West today has largely opposite functions. This becomes particularly striking in the case of what have come to be called mini-nationalisms, in which smaller ethnic or linguistic groups rebel against the nation-states in question. We may refer here to the current movements for autonomy, or even independence, of the Flemings in Belgium, the Basques in Spain or the French Canadians. Another example is the current resurgence of ethnicity in the United States (to the extent that it is a real social movement rather than a concoction of intellectuals and mass media). Modernity has coupled the liberation of the individual with the construction of vast agglomerate structures. Demodernization is directed against the anonymity and abstraction of these structures, *even if the price for this should be less autonomy for the individual.*

In the United States, liberalism as a political ideology has been a major representation of modernizing forces. The self-consciousness of liberals about being in the vanguard of progress is, therefore, perfectly valid as long as one identifies progress with the peculiar structures of modernity. The current crisis of liberalism in this country offers some instructive examples of the concurrence of modernizing and demodernizing impulses in the contemporary situation. Two timely examples from America are the black movement and Women's Liberation.

The notions of social justice propounded by liberalism are distinctively modern in that rights are defined as highly abstract *and* highly individual. The classical American formulation of this can be found in the formula that says that an individual is to be treated fairly "regardless of race, color or creed." The combination of abstraction and individualism in this formula is very important.[12] Demodernizing movements tend to protest against both these aspects. Thus the ideology of the early civil rights movement was clearly liberal in orientation. The rights of the Negro were defended as universal *human* rights, and they pertained to each individual qua individual. The rise of black nationalism in the wake of the civil rights movement has profoundly changed these themes. The formulas of black nationalism are highly concrete and cannot be translated into abstract notions of universal human rights. What is more, the rights in question pertain to the black community as a collective entity rather than to the individual. Indeed, individual success and aspiration are increasingly condemned as a betrayal of the collective effort. These new themes are not only anti-liberal, but they are right in line with the demodernizing impetus under discussion here.

A very similar split may be observed in the movement of Women's Liberation. There is the liberal, and very modern, wing of the movement, which has the basic intention of adding sex to those concrete qualities that the liberal formula of nondiscrimination proposes to ignore. Women are to be treated as individuals and in terms of the abstract rights that pertain to individuals. This wing of Women's Liberation is the ideological correlate of the civil rights movement. It achieved a certain poetic climax in the statement of a young man about his liberated mate: "To me she is just a guy with an extra hole." Other branches of Women's Liberation are much closer ideologically to black nationalism. The concrete particularity of women *as against* men is now emphasized. The rights to be fought for are highly concrete (as against abstract) and they pertain to women as a collectivity (and not to individual women qua individuals). Very much like black nationalism, this new feminism vehemently repudiates the liberal formulas, and indeed seems to be animated by a strong anti-liberal animus. The demodernizing impulse goes a long way to explain these ideological constellations, and also to clarify the liberation that is the avowed aim of these movements.

Other examples could easily be added. To mention only one more, without elaborating on it, the present religious resurgences not only indicate a possible reversal of the secularization trend, but can be understood as a particular manifestation of the demodernizing impulse.

For reasons indicated above, demodernizing themes in the contemporary situation have become concentrated among the youth and crystallized if not institutionalized in the youth culture and in that counterculture which can best be described as a voluntary association of ex-youths heroically refusing to admit their age. We would contend that both youth culture and counterculture can best be understood in terms of demodernizing conscious-ness, and we will look at this in some detail in the next chapter. Here, however, we would like to conclude with one observation: in both youth culture and countercul-ture, in America and in Western Europe, there is a strong identification with the Third World. Imagined peasant tastes are approximated in clothing. Aesthetic and reli-gious expressions have an Asian bias. Political heroes are generally Third World revolutionaries. It is very easy to satirize such upper-middle-class play-acting of the role of peasant. Indeed, it is strongly reminiscent of the shepherd dances performed by Marie Antoinette and her aristo-cratic entourage in the gardens of Versailles.

All the same (and without wanting to take the edge off anyone's satire), a correct intuition is involved in all of this. Youth culture and counterculture are indeed engaged in a rebellion against the same structures of modernity felt as alien impositions in the Third World. The confluence of demodernization and counter-modernization, however ab-surd politically or aesthetically, has a distinctive logic of its own, which is important to understand.

9

Demodernizing Consciousness

The youth culture and the counterculture in contemporary Western societies are complex phenomena that may be viewed from a variety of social-scientific perspectives.[1] For example, it makes sense to look at the youth culture in terms of its function of keeping large numbers of individuals out of the labor market *and* happy (or at least reasonably happy) about this, or, from a Marxist point of view, to understand the counterculture as an escapist response to the frustrations of political conflict. Our analysis here of the youth culture and the counterculture as embodiments of demodernizing consciousness does not necessarily contradict these other interpretations, although perhaps it throws a new and useful light on these phenomena.

To delineate the demodernizing themes in contemporary youth culture and counterculture, we must return to the discussion of the symbolic universe of modernity introduced in Chapter 4, particularly to those elements of it that are intrinsically linked to technological production and bureaucracy. And since the counterculture is essentially the youth culture's parasite, we will refer to both as simply the youth culture.

In enumerating the elements of modernity derived from technological production, we mentioned rationality, specifying that we did not mean the rationality of modern science or philosophy (or any other form of specifically modern *theoretical* rationality), but rather the *functional* rationality imposed by technology upon everyday life. And we showed that bureaucracy imposes a similar if not identical rationality. Logically enough, the youth culture has singled out this type of rationality as a principal foil against which to define itself.

Functional rationality means, above all, the imposition of rational controls over the material universe, over social relations and finally over the self. The youth culture is in rebellion against all three forms. The engineering mentality, which rationally apprehends and manipulates both material and social reality, is denigrated as a perversion that deprives human beings of a "natural" relationship to the world. "Unnatural" control is contrasted with "natural" surrender. Instead of dominating reality, one should "dig" it. Instead of manipulating others, one should "encounter" them. Feeling ("sensitivity," "sensibility") is given priority over rational thought. Indeed, the youth culture has a generalized hostility to all planning, calculation and systematic projects. These are categorized as "uptight" (which is, incidentally, one of the most precisely apt linguistic creations of the youth culture), as against the free-flowing, unconfined spontaneity of "natural" living. This helps to explain a variety of youth-culture patterns in language, gesture and physical accouterments. The imprecision of language, the gangling looseness of gait, the affinity for unrestrained hair and body odor and "unbuttoned" clothes of every sort, all carry meaning as physical expressions of counter-definition. The contrary to "uptightness" is (again, very precisely) to "let it all hang out."

In counter-defining itself as against functional rationality, the youth culture has a strong element of nature worship. The institutions and mental patterns of techno-logical-bureaucratic society are seen as "unnatural" pathologies; the therapy, logically enough, is to get closer to nature. Indeed, a neo-mysticism has emerged in the youth culture in which transcendence of individuality and union with nature (blissful and de-individuating at the same time—the classical combination of all mysticism) are key themes. Sexuality as a process of discovering reality has attained virtually sacramental significance. "Making love" is posited against "making war," the creativity of the natural against the destructive, death-dealing power of the technological-bureaucratic world. Sexual orgasm, the ecstasies of surrender to rock music and the drug experience have in common the quality of de-individuation and liberation from rational controls. They are "mind-blowing" in that they explode that particular "mind" with which one operates in an everyday life shaped by functional rationality.

The implicit anthropology in all of this is quite clear: Underneath the constraining structures of individuality and rationality lies the healing reality of our "natural" being, an *ens realissimum*, which is the object of a quasi-soteriological quest. If there is a certain contradiction between the neo-mystical goal, which is almost by definition elitist, and the mass character of the youth culture, this is not the first time such a contradiction has appeared in the history of man's soteriological quest.

It is important to understand that these themes are rooted in pre-theoretical consciousness—that is, in consciousness prior to any particular theoretical legitimations.[2] Just as it is misleading to deduce modern consciousness from the theories of scientists or philosophers, so it is equally misleading to trace demodernizing consciousness to this or that intellectual theory. The products of intellectuals are mobilized ex post facto to legitimate themes already present in the consciousness of a particular group. Legitimating theories are taken up and discarded again, subject to the vicissitudes of both fashion and ideological need. The underlying social-psychological reality (that which is to be legitimated) has much greater stability. Thus the aforementioned counter-definitions of reality as against the world of functional rationality have been legitimated by a great variety of theories—the anti-"repression" psychologies of Norman O. Brown, R. D. Laing and Wilhelm Reich, the peculiar mixture of psychological and political soteriology of Herbert Marcuse and the Frankfurt School, the ideology of violence as represented by Frantz Fanon or Eldridge Cleaver, the neo-mystical doctrines of Alan Watts and Timothy Leary—and so on.

Some of these theories developed in direct symbiosis with the youth culture itself, in a dialectic between production and audience greatly assisted by the instant-celebrity status provided by modern mass media. Other theories were taken over from quite different sociocultural contexts and (sometimes very selectively) assimilated to the legitimation requirements of the youth culture. The very frequency with which legitimating theories are replaced should alert one to the fact that they are not intrinsic to the phenomenon.

Looking at the contemporary American scene, there are two cultural movements that have a particular affinity with the demodernizing impulse of the youth culture. One is the ecology movement,[3] which both expresses and legitimates the profoundly antitechnological, "naturalistic" animus of the youth culture. At least in the more radical branches of the movement, modern urban, technological society is viewed as a planetary cancer, eating up the life-giving energies of Mother Earth. Salvation is some kind of return to a non-urban, nontechnological way of life, or, failing that, an ongoing struggle to protect whatever is left of the wilderness in the contemporary world. The other movement is the resurgence of occultism, magic and mystical religion (heavily concentrated in the youth culture, though by no means coextensive with it). This has taken a bewildering variety of forms—from astrology to a revival of Satanism, from fascination with ancient Chinese divination techniques to the revival of faith-healing practices in mainstream Christian denominations, and including such properly religious manifestations as Pentecostalism (amazingly insurgent in Roman Catholic milieus), newly aggressive Hindu and Buddhist mysticisms (from Zen to Transcendental Meditation), and the Jesus People. All this becomes much less bewildering as soon as one grasps the counter-definitional aspect of the phenomenon: whatever may divide these movements and groups, they have in common their profound opposition to the definitions of reality that pertain to functional rationality. All of them are thus, at least in part, efforts to cope with the discontents of modernity that they (quite correctly) associate with functional rationality.

Two other themes of the symbolic universe of modernity—componentiality and multi-relationality—are also antagonistic to the youth culture. Indeed, unification (as against componentiality) and simplification (as against multi-relationality) are the key motifs of demodernization embodied in the youth culture.

Componentiality, as we saw earlier, produces a nostalgia for wholeness, unity and comprehensibility.[4] Reality is not to be "chopped up" into discrete units, but to be experienced (in the anthropology of the youth culture, re-experienced) as a unified totality. In the extreme, neo-mystical version, this totalistic experience transcends even the division between self and world, internal and external reality. In the more common and more moderate versions, there is a continuous tendency to bridge separations, to bring together discrepant realms of experience or cognition. Separation, in experience or in thought, is deemed pathology ("schizophrenia"); conversely, unification is "healthy," "natural," even redemptive. On the campus, the aversion to disciplinary specialization (in the radical sense, to any kind of sharp intellectual differentiation) and the desire for "total life experiences" express this theme very well.

One of the most important consequences of componentiality is its effect on the temporal structures of everyday life. The collision between modern and premodern structures of time, which we analyzed in Chapter 6, is repeated—in reverse order, as it were—in the youth culture. Modernity means to live in the time of the clock and the calendar. The former organizes everyday life; the latter makes possible the complex processes we have called life-planning. Both of these levels of modern temporality are pejoratively defined in the youth culture. To organize one's day by the clock offers prima facie evidence of "uptightness"; to organize one's life by the calendar is to be a victim of the "rat race." On both levels, the youth culture posits its *"now!"* against the calculated projections and the delayed gratifications of modern consciousness. In a very fundamental sense, the youth culture is opposed to waiting. In this, incidentally, it differs importantly from most pre-modern cultures: they have great difficulty with life-planning, but most of life consists of waiting; the youth culture, by contrast, can *neither* plan *nor* wait. Thus, while the legitimations of the youth culture's "now" character are sometimes reminiscent of classical mysticism (one may think here, for instance, of Meister Eckhart's category of *"das Nun"*), the everyday reality seems closer to infantile temper tantrums than to the transcendence of time by the great mystics. Once again, the "gentle revolution" of modern childhood is an important factor to consider here.

Closely related to the rejection of life-planning is the rejection of achievement. In America, and especially with those members of the youth culture who have had the benefit of introductory sociology in college, this is interpreted (again, quite accurately) as being directed against the "Protestant ethic." All the virtues of this ethic are, to say the least, suspect as "uptight"; they are attacked as leading to "repression," "alienation," "inauthenticity" and so forth (there is a convenient lexicon of negative categories "at hand" in the youth culture's arsenal of legitimations; in this case, there is a choice of neo-Freudian, Marxist and existentialist categories). The negative definition covers the virtues of hard work, sobriety, saving, even honesty (in its economic component of "an honest day's work"), and, above all, ambition and the desire to achieve status, wealth or power. For the youth culture opposites of these qualities are virtues—"hanging loose," "turning on," giving no thought to the morrow, "working the system" (especially the economic system) and generally disdaining the fruits of systematic ambition. This reversal of values is not only a repudiation of the achievement ethos that has served as a key motivation for individual action in modern society, it is inimical to the very notion of life-planning and to the experience of time that life-planning is based upon. In other words, the youth culture is not only "anti-bourgeois" but, more deeply, demodernizing.

Against the multi-relationality of modernity the youth culture sets an intense desire for simplification. While modern society is characterized by a large number of social relationships, most of them very superficial, the youth culture yearns for small groupings within which relationships will be profound. To use Ferdinand Toennies' terms, youth's aspiration is for *Gemeinschaft* (community), counter-posited against the contemporary realities of *Gesellschaft* (organization). It finds the multiplicity and superficiality of modern social life dehumanizing and, in the last resort, unreal. The individual must learn to penetrate the irreality of these social patterns and attain the capacity to relate to others as "real people"—that is, as unique, deeply significant persons. In the ideal society, as defined (often explicitly, always implicitly) by the youth culture, *all* relations with others would be significant in this sense; if one were to use the terminology of George Herbert Mead, *all* others would be "significant others." Leaving aside the question of whether such a society would ever be possible (or whether, if possible, it would be tolerable), it is clear that even the partial realization, in subcultural enclaves, of such a society faces great difficulties in the contemporary situation. Therefore, the youth culture is saddled with the search for techniques to make such relationships attainable. An important example is the currently fashionable encounter-group movement. The paradox of techniques (the very term "technique" refers to a symbolic universe of engineers and bureaucrats) applied to the attainment of nonfunctional relations with other people points to the inherent difficulty of the demodernizing impulse: One wants to be sensitive to others in the manner of a poet, and one is trained for what purports to be such sensitivity in situations that are planned and manipulated in ready-made packages.

As we have argued before (possibly ad nauseam), the theme of multi-relationality is closely related to the modern dichotomy of the public and private spheres. The demodernizing consciousness of the youth culture, right on cue, is antagonistic to this dichotomy, and thus to the general modern "solution" to the frustrations of multi-relationality. The dichotomy is perceived and condemned as "hypocrisy," in the final analysis as pathology. In the ideal society, as projected by the youth-culture imagery, the dichotomy would be abolished. The individual would be equally "at home" in all sectors of his social experience. In practice, this aspiration manifests itself in positive hostility to privacy. Staying by oneself, keeping apart from the group, and "holding back" in any sense are negatively defined qualities. The virtue is "openness"—from reckless verbal self-revelation to being at ease with physical nakedness. Public copulation and public defecation have served to demonstrate the rejection of the dichotomy on a number of dramatic occasions. The violation of the linguistic tabus of speaking "in public" is a less extreme expression of the same intention. Conversely, the intimacies of the individual's life are (at least ideally) open to a collectivity to which he belongs, if not to the public at large. These aspirations are, of course, most fully approximated in various forms of communal living.

The rejection of the public/private dichotomy was given classical poignancy a few years ago, when a West German *communard* stated to a newspaper reporter who was interviewing him: "I have orgasm problems, and I want the public to take cognizance of this fact." The affinity for "obscene" language can be similarly explained.

Two other themes derived from technological production are "makeability" and progressivity. The youth culture tends to be antagonistic to both. "Makeability" is seen as an attitude of rape, of doing violence to reality. The counter-theme is surrender, letting go, an essentially passive stance toward the world. To the extent that "making" (and not only in the double entendre of American idiom) has been understood as a masculine trait, the youth culture is highly "feminized"—again a characteristic expressed very clearly in its clothing and postures. The youth culture is also antagonistic to the "bigger and better," "onward and upward" thrust of modern consciousness. Progressivity implies aspiration, planning, purposeful action, all themes that are highly suspect. Lately, an idea has appeared in conjunction with the propaganda of the ecology movement that has won instant acclaim within the youth culture—the idea of a "no growth" economy. This idea expresses the stand against progress more clearly than anything else.

The youth culture is also in opposition to the key themes of modern consciousness derived from bureaucracy. Against the central notion of society as a system, and as a system to be tinkered with, the youth culture posits community a social entity to be experienced spontaneously. This is expressed in the conception and practice of spontaneous consent in various youth-culture settings (and by no means only in the "participatory democracy" of politically left groups). Collective action here is understood in organic rather than mechanical terms; community is some kind of animal thing, to be felt, intuited, moved to action by an osmosis of wills rather than by deliberate design. The hostility to rules, regular procedures and indeed to "structures" in general is closely related to this anti-system animus. Once again, we come upon an underlying paradox: The goal is spontaneous social experience. The occasions for such experience, however, are hard to maintain in contemporary society. They must, therefore, be designed—indeed, they must be *engineered*. One of the most dramatic manifestations of this paradox is the economic problem of most youth-culture communes. Whatever the cherished experience for which the commune has been created, its survival is dependent upon some variety of continuous economic maintenance; almost invariably, the activity necessary for the latter collides with the experience that serves as the raison d'être of the commune.

Another essential theme derived from bureaucracy, that of taxonomic order, produces a violent reaction in the context of the youth culture. It has a deeply rooted hostility to "law and order," not just on the obvious level of political controls ("repression"), but with regard to any form of institutional ordering. It sometimes appears as if there were a positive lust for disorder in the youth culture. Order, be it in thought or in social practice, is perceived as dead, life-denying, oppressive. Rebelling against order is, conversely, an affirmation of life and liberty. Cognitively, this rebellion is very similar to the rebellion against componentiality. The animus is against "compartmentalization," "petty distinctions," specialization. In terms of social practice, there is an animus against all kinds of regulation, especially against anything in the way of "standard operating procedures." The nonstandard is the good to be sought. Indeed, the nonstandard becomes the norm. The paradox appears again: Since few individuals have the ingenuity required for innovative thoughts or actions, the allegedly nonstandard becomes itself standardized. The irony of the youth culture is that everyone is supposed to "do his own thing" in dynamic disorder— with the result that almost everyone seems to be doing the same things, and highly predictable things to boot. Apart from members of the armed forces, the proponents of the youth culture are probably the most uniform portion of the population in their clothing—one can spot them, like soldiers, a mile away.

The antagonism against order (specifically, order as associated with bureaucratic regulation) carries over into a broad anti-institutionalism.[5] Every institution, however benign in appearance or intentions, is life-denying and "repressive." The youth culture is thus constantly in search of alternatives to this or that institutional order, be it on campus, in the family, or in the wider political or economic arenas. It has an affinity for dynamism, spontaneity, "movements," all seen in counter-position to the static order of institutions. In all the areas of social life that are under the sway of institutions, the youth culture would like to see unstructured community, spontaneous action, person-to-person encounter. Sociologically, of course, this is impossible (in any human society, not only in a modern one). However, the desire to bring it into being makes it necessary to construct elaborate façades of spontaneity to cover institutional processes. For example, political organizations (such as the "New Politics" caucuses in the Democratic party) that seek support in the youth culture go to considerable lengths to give themselves the look of "movements." Or, for another example, the youth culture has responded well to the practice of disruption—throwing into chaos any particular ordered procedure. Disruption, however, has only limited variability (after all, how many *spontaneous* ways are there of insulting a dean?). Disruption has, therefore, become institutionalized. If one looks at many public gatherings in America today, one is tempted to coin the category of "programmed disruption."[6]

The institutionalization of anti-institutionalism, however, by no means entails the demise of the latter as a theme in consciousness. It persists as a motive for action, sometimes with very real effects in society. The most visible is a recurring (albeit, of necessity, selective) impulse toward insurrection against this or that institutional arrangement. The youth culture, in other words, is "revolution-prone"—very much so on the level of rhetoric, but often to quite an extent on the level of action as well.

The antagonism to institutions logically extends to institutional roles on the level of everyday life. To play a role is, ipso facto, to engage in hypocrisy. The real self (that spontaneous, un-"repressed," to-be-intuited entity) is presumed to lie beneath or beyond all roles, which are masks, camouflage, obstacles to the discovery of the real self. In line with this, there is an affinity for any form of self-denuding, physical as well as verbal.

The concept of the naked self, beyond institutions and roles, as the *ens realissimum* of human being, is at the very heart of modernity. Thus while the rebellion against the bureaucratic structures may be understood as a demodernizing impulse, the anthropological assumptions of the rebellion are profoundly modern. It is here, in our opinion, that we encounter the paradox in its most profound form. The demodernizing impulse of rebellion against the structures of modernity faces a dilemma. *Either* it can continue its assault on institutions in the name of a modern notion of the meta-institutional self— in which case it will, in one way or another, perpetuate the classical modern dichotomy of "unreal institutions"/"real self," thus defeating the original motive for rebellion. *Or* it will create new institutions to which it will ascribe a higher status of reality, in which case (probably at great cost) it will be forced to revise its assumptions about the relationship of self and society. In the former case the demodernizing impulse will become *privatized;* in the latter case it will eventuate in one or another variety of *totalitarianism.* There is, however, the possibility that intermediate solutions will be found to the dilemma.[7]

It is highly significant that the demodernizing impulses of the youth culture have made their appearance at the very center of the most modernized societies. If the global effect of modernization can be described as "homelessness," then the underlying aspiration of demodernization is a quest for new ways of "being at home" in society. Almost all the significant categories for community in the youth culture bear this out. We need mention only "global village," "tribe" and "family," and we cite only the name of Charles Manson, to indicate that this quest for familial at-home-ness is not without some moral ambiguities.

10

The Limits of Demodernization

In the preceding chapter we touched a number of times on certain built-in difficulties for any demodernizing aspirations—built-in in the sense of stemming directly from certain cognitive and psychological presuppositions deeply implanted in the consciousness of the demodernizers themselves. The same point could be made by saying that once established, modern consciousness is rather hard to get rid of. Its definitions of reality and its psychological consequences are dragged along even into the rebellions against it, providing the ironic spectacle of an assault on modernity by people whose consciousness presupposes the same modernity. From the vantage point of our analysis of modern consciousness, we may speak here of intrinsic limits to any demodernizing enterprise. There are also, however, extrinsic limits, that is, limits set not so much by structures of consciousness but by the institutional requirements of contemporary society.

The demodernizing impulse seeks to reverse or transform the technological and bureaucratic determinants of contemporary society. In its more radical form it would like to reorder society by principles that are, by and large, the very opposite of those structures we have described as intrinsic to technological production and bureaucracy. In more moderate versions the demodernizers would like to transform these structures by providing more or less drastic alternatives to the status quo. To use the package concept, demodernization entails taking the packages apart and, in one way or another, depending upon the ideological orientations of the demodernizers, reassembling them in novel ways. Our analysis suggests that demodernization, at least in its more radical manifestations, is faced with very definite limits in any such projects.

These limits are imposed institutionally by the simple fact that short of unspeakable catastrophe, contemporary society cannot divest itself of its technological *or* bureaucratic structures *in toto*. The classical Japanese feat of throwing modernity overboard cannot be repeated. Or rather, if it were repeated, either in the advanced industrial societies or in nearly any part of the Third World today, the result would be untold suffering and even death for millions of people. As we have tried to show, this fact has implications for consciousness as well as for the external order of institutions: if we are "stuck with" technology and bureaucracy, we are *also* "stuck with" those structures of consciousness that are intrinsic to these processes. Put differently, there are certain packages that cannot be taken apart.

An example might make this point more economically. A few years ago the American army, as part of its indoctrination in military neatness, produced a motion picture containing the following sequence. A customer is seen approaching a teller's window in a bank. Behind the window appears a stereotyped hobo with unkempt hair, stubble all over his face, a dirty open shirt, a cigarette dangling from the corner of his mouth. "Would you entrust your money to this man?" asks the announcer. The answer is obvious as the customer in the film retreats from the window with a dismayed expression, clutching his money. "But how about this man?" asks the announcer again as a new teller appears behind the window—well groomed, close-shaven, with clean shirt and tie and an impeccable Chase Manhattan smile on his face.

Let us vary the picture a little. Suppose you are waiting in an airport lounge prior to going on a plane trip and see the pilots walking toward the plane across the tarmac —two stereotyped counterculture types, with shaggy hair and beads, moving loose-limbed to an unheard rock rhythm, one of them fondling a cooing stewardess and the other puffing on a marijuana joint. "Would you want to take a trip in this plane?" The answer, we believe, is obvious—no matter how great your sympathies with the counterculture may be.[1]

It is impossible to fly a commercial airliner safely unless the pilots, and indeed all concerned with the technical aspects of the matter from the Boeing plant to the control towers of the particular route, operate within the structures of a rigidly controlled technological consciousness. To be sure, having long hair or "hanging loose" in one's body movements are not necessarily disqualifications in themselves. But the structures of consciousness symbolized by these "presentations of self" (to use Erving Goffman's phrase) *are* disqualifying. For this reason every halfway nervous airline passenger would like his pilots to

look and act like the pilots on a TWA advertisement—
not because he necessarily shares the aesthetic of the
TWA personnel department, but because he hopes that
the TWA pilots really think the way they look. In other
words, whatever our private "life style," we want commercial airline pilots to be as "square" as they come.

This example is not arbitrary. It points to one particular activity within technological society, but it can
easily be multiplied a thousandfold to cover other activities—activities without which our lives would become unthinkable. Moreover, the example can be extended from
the technological to the bureaucratic area. Indeed, we
can fall back on our corny army movie here. Suppose you
want to make an airline reservation, perhaps a very complicated one, for an important trip. And suppose the man
behind the reservations counter manifests some of the
more visible symptoms of a demodernizing consciousness.
"Would you want to let this man make your travel arrangements?" We daresay that the answer is no—unless,
for reasons of your own, you are prepared to miss your
connections, lose your luggage and arrive at the wrong
destination.

The same example opens up further considerations.
Not everyone in contemporary society is a pilot, and even
a pilot does other things in life besides fly planes. What
are the implications of these two obvious facts?

Not everyone is a pilot: by extension, not everyone is
directly engaged in the maintenance of the central technological and bureaucratic machineries of modern society.
Conversely, not everyone is equally prone to demodernizing impulses. At least as far as America is concerned, the
phenomena of demodernization discussed in the preceding chapter appear to be heavily concentrated in specific
sections of the population.[2] What evidence we have on

this suggests that the more radical aspects of the youth culture and the so-called counterculture are mainly located within the confines of the college-educated upper middle class. Lower-middle-class and working-class young people, while they may exhibit some of the external accouterments of the youth culture, seem to be much less infused with its demodernizing consciousness. Especially are they less likely to have abandoned the achievement aspirations of the Protestant ethic, and therefore they are much less likely to "drop out" of the conventional career system into some countercultural pattern of life. Long hair or not, most of them appear to remain emphatically within the "rat race."

If this is so, demodernization relates in an interesting way to social mobility. Put simply: as upper-middle-class individuals "drop out" of careers to which their class background would previously have pointed them, positions will open up to be filled by individuals from different class backgrounds. Demodernizing movements in the upper reaches of the class system accelerate social mobility from the lower reaches, where demodernization impulses are weaker or altogether absent. The positions in question are, of course, primarily in those technological and bureaucratic occupations that the ethos of the youth culture and counterculture disdains. Such occupations are in the natural sciences and engineering, in business administration or government service, and other activities that could well be summed up as "minding the shop"—ipso facto "uptight," "uncreative," "square" occupations. Upper-middle-class individuals have been moving out of these occupations to the extent that demodernization has converted them to other aspirations, leaving openings for the unconverted from other classes.[3]

Some of the results of this can already be seen in the

corporations and in government (most dramatically in the military), where recruiters have turned to new and, from their point of view, more "vigorous" strata of the population. The scenario is, once more, paradoxical: demodernization, by facilitating social mobility, indirectly serves the vitality of the modern structures aganst which its rebellion is directed.

The scenario, of course, makes some assumptions that cannot be tested at this juncture. Mainly it assumes that the present class alignment of demodernization will continue in the future. This assumption is far from secure. If our analysis of the relationship of specific middle-class patterns (especially the patterns of childhood we have called the "gentle revolution") to the discontents of modernity is correct, then the present class focus of demodernization is only what we would expect. We have found, however, that patterns originating within the middle class have been pushing beyond their original sociocultural location. This can be seen quite clearly in child-rearing patterns. Thus the lower reaches of the class system are by no means immune to the demodernization impulse; their present immunity is, in all likelihood, a relative one. If this immunity should break down completely, a situation might arise in which there would be, literally, no one left to "mind the shop." In that case, far more radically than in our foregoing discussion, modernity would reveal itself as its own gravedigger.

Because of the unthinkability of divesting society of its technological and bureaucratic underpinnings, however, we are very skeptical of such a development. The results would be so threatening that, long before the final catastrophe, society would be compelled to take countermeasures. Very possibly these would take highly coercive forms. In other words, those still committed to "minding the shop" would have to take drastic steps to protect that enterprise from collapse. In all likelihood they (whoever "they" may be at that point) would gain popular support for their measures to the precise degree that broad masses of people start envisaging the disappearance of modern amenities to which they have grown accustomed. Thus, despite the uncertainties, we are quite sanguine about the chances of the technological-bureaucratic structures solving their recruitment problems.

Generally speaking, social institutions are more resilient than they appear to be during periods of transition and crisis. This is particularly true of the technological and bureaucratic institutions of a modern society. Intellectuals are prone to detect signs of imminent disaster in society on the basis of disturbances that, at times, may be quite superficial. Disturbances are always highly visible, doubly so in an era of instant mass communication, the media of which have a vested interest in the cataclysmic. Much less visible, and much less media-covered, are the processes of continuity, stability and readjustment. We strongly suspect that such is the case in contemporary society, especially in the United States, where intellectuals' prophecies of doom have been the conventional wisdom for the past few years.

On the other hand, the conviction held by any significant portion of the population that their institutions are moving toward collapse is a factor that could gain autonomous power in itself. Put differently, whatever the institutional processes of a society, they interact continuously with the definitions of reality operative in that society. The question eventually is a political one: Who has the power to make particular definitions of reality "stick"? At the present moment in American society, the propaganda of doom has had a considerable edge for a few years, not only in the limited milieu of intellectuals' coteries but in the mass media of communication. Thus a "failure of nerve" about the viability of the institutional order can not only be seen in the defeatist and sometimes even gleefully self-castigating mood of intellectuals and their opinion organs, but is also reflected in public-opinion data referring to much broader samples of the population. Some of the foregoing scenarios will depend to a large extent on whether counter-definitions of reality succeed in establishing themselves in the future and what kind of political power is available to provide plausibility for such counter-definitions.

Be this as it may, it seems clear to us that demodernization in advanced industrial societies has limits that may be shifting but are nonetheless quite firm. To repeat, these limits are grounded in the necessity of maintaining the fundamental technological and bureaucratic machineries of the society. This means that demodernization, and the social constellations created by it, will be parasitical upon the structures of modernity. Their most likely social form is that of subcultures, enclaves, "reservations." Their existence in any of these forms depends not only on the tolerance of the larger society but to a large degree on subsidization by that society. This, of course, is emphatically clear in the case of the youth culture and somewhat less so in the case of the counterculture (insofar as the latter contains adults rather than young people). The youth culture maintains itself on the subsidies of "straight" society—on parents' checks, welfare mechanisms of the state, scholarships, subsidized college fees and the like. Even those countercultural milieus that, seemingly, have divorced themselves from the "straight" economy are indirectly subsidized as well. Countercultural communes may support themselves by sandal-making or similar artistic endeavors, or even by amateur farming. But this type of economic activity is dependent on the existence of the other, "serious" economy, which is affluent enough to afford such nonproductive activities and which supports the infrastructure of public services (from electricity to medical care) without which the countercultural enclaves would descend into abject misery.

It should be emphasized that the term "parasitical" is not intended in a pejorative sense. It simply describes the economic and social relationship of dependency. As soon as this relationship is recognized, however, some of the self-definitions of the youth culture and counterculture as autonomous ("liberated") zones within society lose credibility. As we have argued, the zones cannot be significantly enlarged without endangering the survival of everybody (the "liberated" as well as the "unliberated") in the society. Barring significant enlargement, however, the "autonomy" of these zones resembles that of Indian reservations—or, to use a more timely Third World illustration, of "Bantustans." Indeed, the political logic may not be too dissimilar. The "savages" are allowed to perform their dances without disturbance, may even be subsidized in this performance (perhaps as a tourist attraction) and permitted a great measure of self-administration in their designated locations. They are ipso facto controlled politically and effectively prevented from having an influence on the "civilized" sectors of the society. Their inhabitants may be described as "licensed barbarians"— an image hardly corresponding to the high self-esteem in which these groups hold themselves, particularly in America.

There is another notion current in the counterculture today that ought to be mentioned here. This is the notion that *because of* the advanced technology of modern society, "alternative life styles" may become dominant. This implies that the material needs of society can increasingly be taken care of by automation, by cybernetic networks, and by similar technological wonders requiring no or little human personnel for their operation. While these automated systems are working away by themselves, people will be free to devote themselves to various "creative" pursuits. Bureaucracy in particular is to be done in by such devices. It requires little sociological sophistication to see that this scenario is illusionary. Even if such automated technology could be set up efficiently (paradoxically again, this assumption requires an inordinate amount of faith in the powers of technology), there would still be the crucial political question of who would control the automated system. On the basis of all the preceding considerations, we think that it would *not* be the "creative" people who have turned away from these mundane concerns. Most likely, it would be a technological and political elite with a consciousness diametrically opposed to that of the counterculture. Far from making possible the envisaged "liberation," this sort of technological automatism would very probably provide the foundation for permanent totalitarian rule of the very few over the many. The ensuing society would have the look of a gigantic Skinner Box.

To return to our aeronautical example. A pilot does other things besides fly planes. While flying his plane, a pilot must operate within a time structure that is rigidly and totally modern. He must operate, in other words, on a time in which measures down to seconds matter greatly. There is no reason to assume that he continues to be on this time when he goes home to his family. Thus (to take the extreme but obvious case) we may hope that he is *not* watching his chronometer while he is in bed with his wife. To take up terms used earlier in our argument, there is stoppage between the pilot's directly technological activity and other areas of his social life; conversely, there may be considerable carry-over from the former to the latter (for all we know, there are particularly dedicated types who *never* take off their chronometers).

These considerations open up scenarios less radical than those discussed above. If full commitment to the demodernizing values of the counterculture is somehow reminiscent of a fervent Puritanism, it makes sense to look at the "halfway covenant" of the less fervent adherents. We see this as a position, somewhere between full-time "dropping out" into a countercultural enclave and the purely superficial exhibition of countercultural symbols. That is, it is a position "halfway" between the sandal-making denizen of a commune and the Madison Avenue executive with sideburns. Thus it is possible that the youth culture and counterculture will have modifying effects on the overall culture—hardly a process to be described as "greening," but perhaps as adding a touch of "green" here and there. These modifications may range from rather irrelevant changes in conduct (the Madison Avenue executive, say, adds a couple of positions from the Kama Sutra to his amorous repertoire) to significant transformations of some social institutions. For example, the rapid diffusion through American colleges and universities of a youth-culture antagonism toward precise evaluations of academic achievement is likely to have quite significant consequences—not only on the academic institutions themselves, but on the institutions (business, science, government and so on) that previously relied upon the now-suspect evaluations. One quite plausible scenario here would be the metamorphosis of colleges (at least on the undergraduate level) into temporary youth-culture "Bantustans," which would necessitate the creation or reshaping of other institutional processes for the purpose of evaluation. College students might be allowed to rate themselves on their mastery of the I Ching, but some other agency would have to make sure that those of them who become, say, engineers know how to build a bridge that doesn't collapse in a week. Such a shifting in institutional functions could hardly be described as the establishment of a new culture, but it would entail social changes of considerable importance.

The modification of the sociocultural situation by demodernizing impulses also raises the possibility of pluralistic developments in various areas. One such area may very likely be education.[4] The technological and bureaucratic machineries of contemporary society will continue to require educational arrangements that will of necessity be dominated by specifically modern structures of consciousness for the replenishing of their staffs. But the technological and bureaucratic machineries will not require staffs that include the total population. Indeed, with the advances of automation in economic activities proper and in various administrative networks, the need for trained personnel in these areas may shrink considerably. There would then be no pragmatic reasons to prevent the growth of educational institutions whose purpose is *not* to train individuals for technologically or bureaucratically relevant competence but for any number of educational goals that would seem outlandish to most educators today.

One might even envisage a situation in which there would be parallel career systems in society, some within the technological-bureaucratic structures, others outside them. Each system would have its own educational institutions, its own hierarchy of status (quite different from the hierarchy of any other system), and, naturally, its own package of cognitive and normative definitions of reality. We cannot deal here with the question of how such a society would hold together politically or morally.[5] One thing, however, seems clear: pluralism along these lines (even on a much more modest scale than just suggested) presupposes a cultural climate of tolerance. This, in turn, presupposes a high degree of freedom from the most pressing economic concerns. In other words, such pluralism is conceivable only in an affluent economic situation. Almost certainly it also requires a growing economy; the "no growth" economy frequently proposed in the propaganda of the counterculture would very likely spell its demise. In a stagnant economic situation, competition for the available positions and benefits would become fierce, and there would be much greater reluctance to subsidize deviant subcultures—except perhaps as "Bantustans" in the most literal sense of coercively segregated slums.

It follows that the limits for comparable modifications of modern structures are narrower in the Third World. There the prognosis for counter-modernization is more negative than the above for demodernization. This is so despite the fact that the modern or modernizing structures in the Third World today coexist with much larger entities of traditional, as yet non-modern patterns of culture and social life. Most Third World societies find themselves under extreme economic and social pressures, some of which we touched upon in Part II. In such a situation there is the overriding compulsion to mobilize, as far as possible, the entire population for purposes of development. There is much less leeway for experimentation with pluralistic options and less tolerance for what will appear to those in charge of the society as expensive luxuries or worse. As we saw in Chapter 7, there are powerful ideologies in the Third World that seek to control development in terms of values not derived from the modern West, and concomitant government policies seeking to devise alternatives to Western institutional patterns. These ideologies and policies, however, all exist in a context of (often desperate) economic urgency. The practical options for their realization have, therefore, tended to be narrow. For example, the kind of pluralism in the area of education mentioned above has a greater likelihood of being realized in North rather than in Latin America.[6]

On the other hand, Third World countries do provide a variety of situations in which innovative policies are being tried out, and in which modern institutions are more or less new and thus not as burdened with structural ossification as they are in advanced industrial societies. There may, after all, be something to what Thorstein Veblen called the "advantage of coming late" (which the Dutch historian Jan Romein put even more optimistically as the "leap of the retarded"). Given clear-sighted political leadership, and also a situation in which the pressure of immediate necessities is sufficiently under control to provide some flexibility in policy, Third World societies may be in a position to learn from the history of modern institutions in the West and to innovate accordingly.

Nevertheless, there is ground for skepticism about what may be called the Zionisms regarding the Third World now current in Western countries—that is, the fervent expectation that somewhere in the Third World the solutions for the major problems of all contemporary societies are being hammered out. The particular targets of these Zionisms shift frequently, as this or that Third World country (usually one under an avowedly revolutionary or "left" regime) either raises or disappoints the expectations of its Western admirers. The image of the country in question held by its "Zionists" in the West frequently bears little resemblance to its empirical reality. Thus, for instance, Western "Maoism" makes little sense if seen as a response to the realities of Communist China; it should rather be seen against the background of specifically Western discontents and aspirations. The consequence of this, of course, is that all these Zionisms are endemically precarious ideologies, especially when their proponents obtain firsthand experience of their particular "Zion." We have said that the demodernizers' interest in the Third World is based on a correct intuition. We should add that this intuition is only rarely coupled with sound knowledge or a sober appraisal of the available options.

But one thing should now be amply clear: if counter-modernization and demodernization have their limits, so, emphatically, does modernization. A totally modern society would be a science-fiction nightmare. Long before such a culmination is reached, the discontents of modernity would rise to an intensity that requires modifications of the institutional structures. The transition that all advanced industrial societies are now passing through can, in large measure, be understood as a quest for viable modifications of this sort. There is good reason to think that an increasing number of people have become dissatisfied with the classical "solution" of dichotomizing their social experience between the public and private spheres. There are strenuous efforts afoot to modify the institutions of the public sphere so as to make it more responsive to the needs and aspirations that were originally located (and, to a point, satisfied) in private life.

Anyone who claims to know the outcome of these efforts is foolhardy indeed, regardless of whether his focus is on the advanced industrial societies or the Third World. We contend, however, that any effort seeking alternatives to existing institutional patterns can only benefit from an awareness of the probable limits of such an enterprise, and we believe that these limits are to be sought, in the main, in the technological and bureaucratic institutions of modern society and the structures of consciousness that intrinsically pertain to them. We are not antagonistic to the hope that these limits are broad enough to allow for some alternatives that may be genuinely new.

Conclusion:

Political Possibilities

It is customary today to demand that every social-scientific analysis be looked at in terms of its political implications. Certain aspects of this demand are reprehensible. Often it expresses an ideological fanaticism, which cannot tolerate ambiguity and which must immediately assign a stamp of blessing or damnation to everything and everyone coming to its attention. At other times it represents an inability to grasp the value of the theoretical attitude, a crass impatience about the inevitable hiatus between insight and action. We hold no brief for these aberrations. Ideological fanaticism has no place in the social sciences. Nor can the social sciences be expected to provide instant and continuous answers to Lenin's classical question, *What is to be done?* Yet, on a deeper level, perhaps the demand is justified. The basic questions to which the social scientist addresses himself are questions that involve inordinate amounts of human anguish and human hope. There is something obscene about the social scientist who pursues his inquiries in a stance of aloofness from this anguish and hope. It follows that there is a political obligation to the craft of social science. There are different responses to the obligation, and it should not be defined dogmatically or mechanically. There may be individuals who can in good conscience refuse to respond, claiming a right to devote themselves *sine ira et studio* to this or that politically irrelevant investigation. Such individuals are probably few, however, and such a claim would be very hard to sustain for the topics discussed in this book.

Yet the political implications of our argument are neither obvious nor unambiguous. Even the authors are not at all of one mind concerning the political lessons to be drawn. For example, there has been repeated mention of socialism in the preceding pages. In some places our discussion of socialism could be interpreted as affirming its inevitability (at least in the Third World), in other places as a sharp critique of the intellectual assumptions of socialist programs. Yet one can proceed from our argument and arrive at either a socialist or a non-socialist position regarding the feasible and desirable future of modern societies. The one sure conclusion that our argument offers is that socialism cannot be per se a solution to the intrinsic discontents of modernity. This does, indeed, offer a challenge to the Marxist understanding of "alienation." However, there are quite different grounds on which one might arrive at a socialist position, such as, say, an economic analysis of the international capitalist system, or, for that matter, a meta-scientific conviction of the requirements of distributive justice.

Especially in the later part of this book we have repeatedly discussed questions of limits. We contend that such discussion is important not only for its analytical but also for its political uses. The social sciences cannot, and should not, offer ideological or policy unanimity. They can, however, indicate certain parameters on which individuals with discrepant ideological or pragmatic interests can rationally agree. Such a conception of the proper task of the social sciences is often decried today as "neutralism," while its proponents are attacked either as ideologists hiding their true colors or as people bereft of the passions of political engagement. This is not the place to take up once again the old quarrel about the objectivity of the social sciences. We can only reaffirm our conviction that the differentiation between science and ideology continues to be valid and eminently important. We will, however, allow ourselves one brief comment on the notion that intellectual detachment is identical with lack of moral passion. This represents a rather deplorable *machismo* of the mind. It fails to understand that passion consists of both control and surrender, of ice as well as fire, and that, indeed, the true test of passion in politics as well as in other areas is its capacity to endure distance from that which it seeks to embrace.

Whatever the parameters mentioned above may be, in the final analysis it will come down to a question of values. Thus we have tried, as it were, to set up the parameters of modern "homelessness." What one will want "to be done" about all this will depend on whether one attaches greater value to the individual's autonomy or to his security, to freedom or to belonging. We know of no way in which the social sciences, using their own cognitive tools, can decide this issue. Yet a good many political implications of our argument will hinge on the decision, not least the question of how acceptable the modern dichotomization of social life into a public and a private sphere is.

If the passion with which one engages oneself in the struggles of one's time can consist of both ice and fire, then surely sociological analysis belongs to the icy part. Sociology is essentially a debunking discipline. It dissects, uncovers, only rarely inspires. Its genius is very deeply negative, like that of Goethe's Mephistopheles who describes himself as a "spirit that ever says no." To try to change this character is to destroy whatever usefulness sociology may have—especially its moral and political usefulness, which comes from being held in balance, simultaneously and within the mind of the same person, with the affirmations of moral passion and humane engagement. Therefore, we offer no apology for the frequently negative tone of our argument.

It has not been our intention to deprecate the efforts to change and humanize the structures of modernity. On the contrary, we are strongly committed to such efforts. We are convinced, in particular, of the necessity to seek alternatives to many existing structures, on the levels of both institutions and consciousness. Such a search for alternatives, however, crucially involves the question of limits that we have raised. Everyone with a little imagination can think up alternative worlds. He who would be politically relevant must continually ask himself which of these worlds are possible.

We are, for example, very much in sympathy with the theme of participation, which we see as closely linked to the discontents of modernity. In the Third World this theme is part of the urge to be liberated from structures of exploitation and misery. In the advanced industrial societies, it comes out of the protest against the increasing domination of wide areas of life by the technological and bureaucratic institutions. The theme of participation can be embraced as redemption or rejected as romantic illusion. We suggest an approach that skirts these polarities. We also suggest that such an approach is very badly needed today.

The social sciences seem to be haunted by the opposing images of B. F. Skinner and Che Guevara. On the one hand, there is the continuing appeal of a pedantic scientism, which either has no utopian imagination at all or, much worse, produces utopias of its own that make the blood curdle. On the other hand, there is the powerful appeal of messianic utopias, most of them spurred by the heady rhetoric of revolution and violence. Interestingly enough, both attitudes seem to have a marked affinity for totalitarian solutions to the problems of contemporary society. Perhaps there is an intrinsic connection between cognitive totalism and political totalitarianism: the mind that can only tolerate *one* approach to understanding reality is the same kind of mind that must impose *one* all-embracing structure of power if it ever gets into the position of doing so. At that point, it seems to matter little whether the enterprise started out in ice or in fire. What we are suggesting here could be described as the possibility of a *pedantic utopianism*. If this book has a hidden ambition, it is to make a small contribution to this possibility—as both a social-scientific and a political possibility.

Notes

INTRODUCTION

1 On the various conceptualizations of modernization and development, the reader may first want to look at some of the bibliographical compilations. *Cf.* Jacques Austruy (ed.), *Le scandale du développement* (Paris, Marcel Rivière, 1968), a curious combination of a sharp critique of the current concept of development and a well-compiled bibliography; John Brode (ed.), *The Process of Modernization—An Annotated Bibliography* (Cambridge, Mass., Harvard University Press, 1969); René Koenig (ed.), *Aspekte der Entwicklungsssoziologie* (Cologne, Westdeutscher Verlag, 1969). The articles on modernization by Daniel Lerner and James Coleman in the *International Encyclopedia of the Social Sciences* (New York, Macmillan, 1968) are useful for purposes of orientation, as is the excellent volume of essays edited by Myron Weiner, *Modernization* (New York, Basic Books, 1966). Probably the most important single book on the subject in American sociology is Marion Levy's *Modernization and the Structure of Societies* (Princeton, N.J., Princeton University Press, 1966), which represents an approach derived from structural-functional theory. For a useful overview from a historian's viewpoint, *cf.* C. E. Black, *The Dynamics of Modernization* (New York, Harper & Row, 1966). For an example of the Marxist critique of development in its Latin American form, *cf.* Armando Cordova and Hector Silva Michelena, *Aspectos teoricos del subdesarrollo* (Caracas, Universidad Central de Venezuela, 1967).

2 Marion Levy, *Modernization: Latecomers and Survivors* (New York, Basic Books, 1972).

3 Peter Berger and Thomas Luckmann, *The Social Construction of Reality* (Garden City, N.Y., Doubleday, 1966). This book contains detailed references to the sources used for this reformulation of the sociology of knowledge, and we limit ourselves here to this general reference.

4 We would cite here the works of Alex Inkeles and Joseph Kahl. To a large extent the same point can be made with regard to Marion Levy and other approaches derived from structural-functionalism.

5 The works of Margaret Mead, Abram Kardiner and David Mc-Clelland may be cited here.

6 In the social sciences in the United States, the Marxist approach to our topic has been strongest among economists, as in the work of Paul Baran. In Latin America, by contrast, Marxism is the predominant framework for the approach to the topic by social scientists in general.

CHAPTER 1

1 This is what Thorstein Veblen called the "discipline of the machine." *Cf.* Max Lerner (ed.), *The Portable Veblen* (New York, Viking Press, 1948), pp. 335 ff.

2 This term, hardly an aesthetically pleasing contribution to the language of social science, was arrived at reluctantly. We first used "atomism" instead, but discarded this in view of its undesirable philosophical connotations.

3 The importance of "the private sphere" as a novel formation of modern society has been especially stressed in recent German sociology. *Cf.* Arnold Gehlen, *Die Seele im technischen Zeitalter* (Hamburg, Rowohlt, 1957).

4 This was one of the key characteristics that Veblen ascribed to engineers, and the reason for the high hopes he held for the political importance of this group. Eric Hoffer, in his various works, has strongly emphasized (and, incidentally, glorified) the same characteristic as far as ordinary American workers are concerned.

5 *Cf.*, for example, Lloyd Warner and J. O. Low, *The Social System of the Modern Factory* (New Haven, Yale University Press, 1947); Delbert Miller and William Form, *Industrial Sociology* (New York, Harper, 1964). The importance of personal relationships for efficient work performance was the germinal insight, beginning with Elton Mayo and his associates, of the "human relations" movement in industry. *Cf.* William Whyte, *Men at Work* (Homewood, Ill., Dorsey, 1961).

6 "Anonymity" is here understood in the sense of Alfred Schutz, with the implications for the typification of others developed by him.

7 This feature is related to what Robert Merton has called "anticipatory socialization."

8 Both George Herbert Mead and Alfred Schutz have shown that *some* degree of self-anonymization, and thus of self-typification, is neces-

sary for participation in any ongoing social experience. What is peculiar to the case under discussion is the *degree* of self-anonymization.

9 This is an amplification, by way of phenomenological description, of what Erving Goffman has called "role distance."

10 The reason for this one-sided application of the notion of alienation is, of course, its origin in the philosophical anthropology of Marxism, which legitimates the definition of anonymized identity as "less real." Whatever may be the philosophical merits of this position, it can be less than helpful in interpreting particular empirical situations.

11 An excellent example of the carry-over of psychological "engineering" from the world of work to private life is what in German is aptly called *Freizeitgestaltung*, the systematic organization and administration of leisure time. In content this ranges over a broad field of conduct—material consumption, hobbies, sexuality and so on. An analysis of "the vacation," as a peculiarly modern social *and* psychological phenomenon, would be very revealing in this frame of reference.

12 It will be clear that, in saying the above, we part company with the prevailing Marxist interpretations of alienation.

13 This view corresponds to Max Weber's concept of "elective affinity."

CHAPTER 2

1 As in the preceding chapter, we have tried here to describe certain structures of consciousness from our own knowledge, rather than to present a summation of empirical studies bearing on them. At the same time, it will be clear that our own knowledge has a "background" of such studies. We have been particularly influenced by Max Weber's theory of bureaucracy and by subsequent sociological approaches to this phenomenon. On the former, *cf.* Hans Gerth and C. Wright Mills (eds.), *From Max Weber* (New York, Oxford University Press, 1958), pp. 196 ff. For good examples of the latter, *cf.* Peter Blau, *The Dynamics of Bureaucracy* (Chicago, University of Chicago Press, 1955), and Michel Crozier, *The Bureaucratic Phenomenon* (Chicago, University of Chicago Press, 1964).

2 This term was coined by Talcott Parsons.

3 This was brought out very nicely in Robert Merton's theory of bureaucracy. *Cf.* his *Social Theory and Social Structure* (Glencoe, Ill., Free Press, 1957), pp. 199 f.

4 Another Parsonian term, "functional specificity," applies to this trait of bureaucracy.

5 This term is taken from Erving Goffman.

CHAPTER 3

1 For earlier treatments of the notion of pluralization, with special emphasis on its effects on religion, *cf.* Peter Berger, *The Sacred Canopy*

(Garden City, N.Y., Doubleday, 1967), and Thomas Luckmann, *The Invisible Religion* (New York, Macmillan, 1967). The concept of social life-world, as indicated before, derives from Alfred Schutz.

2 As previously mentioned, this aspect has been of particular interest to recent German sociology, and we are particularly indebted in this to the work of Arnold Gehlen.

3 Both Max Weber and Georg Simmel, in their classic studies of urban life, have emphasized the aspect of pluralization (though, of course, they did not use this term). We want to link this conceptualization with the sociological understanding of modern communications.

4 This statement is not intended to contradict the findings of child psychology as to the importance of a safe and coherent social milieu for the individual's early development. The experience of a plurality of reality definitions does not *necessarily* contradict this psychological requirement. On the other hand, it is quite likely that such pluralization introduces instability on various levels of "personality," also in a psychiatrically relevant sense.

5 Once more, we find this term of Robert Merton's very useful for our considerations.

6 For an earlier treatment of this, *cf.* Peter Berger and Hansfried Kellner, "Marriage and the Construction of Reality," *Diogenes*, Summer 1964.

7 *Cf.* Alfred Schutz, *Collected Papers*, Vol. I (The Hague, Nijhoff, 1962), pp. 69 ff.

8 *Cf.* Peter Berger, "Identity as a Problem in the Sociology of Knowledge," *European Journal of Sociology*, VII (1966).

9 This aspect is closely related, not only to Merton's aforementioned concept, but also to David Riesman's of the "other-directed" character. For a comparison between this identity type and the one prevailing in pre-modern societies, *cf.* Daniel Lerner, *The Passing of Traditional Society* (Glencoe, Ill., Free Press, 1958).

10 If one gives credence to the theory of identity derived from George Herbert Mead (as we would), one is compelled to say that, in a very basic way, people in *all* societies have always been "other-directed" and therefore "open-ended." What is peculiar about modern identity is the *degree* of this—which, we contend, is so much greater as to constitute a qualitative change.

11 On this point we are greatly indebted to Arnold Gehlen, especially to his conception of the "subjectivization" of modern man. *Cf.* his *Die Seele des Menschen im technischen Zeitalter* (Hamburg, Rowohlt, 1957).

12 This term derives from William James.

13 For earlier statements of this, *cf.* Thomas Luckmann and Peter Berger, "Social Mobility and Personal Identity," *European Journal of Sociology*, V (1964), and Peter Berger, "Towards a Sociological Understanding of Psychoanalysis," *Social Research*, Spring 1965.

14 Helmut Schelsky has called this the propensity of modern man for *Dauerreflektion*.

15 It is in the context of similar considerations that Luckmann

(*op. cit.*) has analyzed personal autonomy as a key value in contemporary society.

16 For a much fuller treatment of this, see the references given in the first note to this chapter.

EXCURSUS

1 Cited in J. Huizinga, *The Waning of the Middle Ages* (New York, Doubleday-Anchor, 1954), p. 33 [my italics].

2 J. K. Campbell, *Honour, Family and Patronage* (Oxford 1964).

3 *Ibid.* pp. 271 ff.

4 Norbert Elias, *Der Prozess der Zivilisation* (Bern, Francke, 1969).

5 Cervantes, *Don Quixote*, trans. by Walter Starkie (New York, New American Library, 1964), I: 25, p. 243.

6 Cervantes, *op. cit.*, II: 74.

7 Shakespeare, *Henry IV*, Part I, V: 1.

8 Arnold Gehlen, *Moral und Hypermoral* (Frankfurt, Athenäum, 1969).

9 Anton Zijderveld, *The Abstract Society* (New York, Doubleday, 1970).

CHAPTER 4

1 The concept of package was coined by Ivan Illich, who uses it in a slightly different sense.

2 The concept of carrier (*Träger*) is taken from Max Weber.

3 See particularly Emile Durkheim, *The Division of Labor in Society* (Glencoe, Ill., Free Press, 1960); Ferdinand Toennies, *Community and Society* (East Lansing, Mich., Michigan State University Press, 1957); Max Weber, *Economy and Society* (New York, Bedminster Press, 1968); Talcott Parsons, *Structure and Process in Modern Societies* (Glencoe, Ill., Free Press, 1960), and *Societies: Evolutionary and Comparative Perspectives* (Englewood Cliffs, N.J., Prentice-Hall, 1966); Marion Levy, *Modernization and the Structure of Societies* (Princeton, N.J., Princeton University Press, 1966), and *Modernization: Latecomers and Survivors* (New York, Basic Books, 1972).

4 *Cf.* Brigitte Berger, *Societies in Change* (New York, Basic Books, 1971).

5 See especially Max Weber, *The Protestant Ethic and the Spirit of Capitalism* (New York, Scribner, 1958).

6 *Cf.* Thomas Luckmann and Peter Berger, "Social Mobility and Personal Identity," *European Journal of Sociology*, Fall 1964.

7 The term "mobility," in this sense, has been used by Daniel Lerner in his *The Passing of Traditional Society* (Glencoe, Ill., Free Press, 1958).

8 Fritz Machlup, *The Production and Distribution of Knowledge in the United States* (Princeton, N.J., Princeton University Press, 1962).

John Kenneth Galbraith's notion of the "technostructure" refers to the same "elite of knowledge."

9 Ivan Illich has made a plausible case for seeing the school as a key institution in modern society (and, in his view, a very nefarious one). See his *Deschooling Society* (New York, Harper & Row, 1971).

10 We have deliberately avoided here the question as to whether, given a certain degree of "development" in the area of technological production, a new phenomenon of "post-industrial society" emerges that must be distinguished from the preceding "industrial society." While there can be no doubt about the reality of the new facts subsumed under the former term, we wonder whether the difference between these two societal types has not been exaggerated, especially since the "post-industrial" constellations continue to be dependent upon an industrial system sustaining them. Be this as it may, a view of "development" in terms of a continuum permits different interpretations of this matter. For an excellent summary of the problem, see Daniel Bell, "The Post-Industrial Society: The Evolution of an Idea," *Survey*, Spring 1971.

11 Theorists of bureaucracy have referred to this variant in terms of "open" and "closed" systems. *Cf.* Philip Selznick, "Foundations of the Theory of Organization," in Amitai Etzioni (ed.), *A Sociological Reader on Complex Organizations* (New York, Holt, Rinehart & Winston, 1969), pp. 26 ff.

12 *Cf.* Peter Berger and Thomas Luckmann, *The Social Construction of Reality* (Garden City, N.Y., Doubleday-Anchor, 1967), pp. 92 ff.

13 Claude Lévi-Strauss has used this term in a completely different sense.

14 Alfred Schutz's ideas concerning the paramount status of the "world of working" may be fruitfully related here to the Marxian conception of the anthropological significance of "labor."

15 See especially Alfred Schutz, *Collected Papers, I* (The Hague, Nijhoff, 1962), pp. 207 ff.

16 The term "role distance" is taken from Erving Goffman.

17 In German this theme is well expressed by the two terms *Rechtsstaat* (a political system based on law) and *Rechtsmittelstaat* (a political system based on legally proper procedures).

18 *Cf.* Talcott Parsons, *The Social System* (Glencoe, Ill., Free Press, 1951), *passim*.

CHAPTER 5

1 See Hortense Powdermaker, *Copper Town* (New York, Harper & Row, 1965). On the relationship of economic development and modernization generally, *cf.*, for instance, A. N. Agarwala and S. P. Singh (eds.), *The Economics of Underdevelopment* (New York, Oxford University Press, 1968), and Helio Jaguaribe, *Economic and Political Development* (Cambridge, Mass., Harvard University Press, 1968).

2 See J. C. Mitchell, *African Urbanization* (Lusaka, Rhodes-Livingstone Communications, 1954), and Powdermaker, *op. cit.*

3 See Powdermaker, *op. cit.*

4 See H. Dunlop, *The African Factory Worker* (London, Oxford University Press, 1950); R. Maistriaux, *L'intelligence et le charactère* (Paris, Presses Universitaires de France, 1959).

5 The foremost proponent of the achievement-motive theory has been David McClelland. *Cf.* his *The Achieving Society* (New York, Free Press, 1967) and (with David Winter) *Motivating Economic Achievement* (New York, Free Press, 1969).

6 *Cf.* Maistriaux, *op. cit.*; Jacques Binet, *Psychologie économique africaine* (Paris, Payot, 1970); Guy Hunter, *The New Societies of Tropical Africa* (New York, Praeger, 1964), especially Part II. The following passage is a good summation of findings in this area: "The African as an employee . . . has small choice but to accept, without adequate understanding, the conditions imposed on him from without. He has little idea of the value of conforming to a schedule, of the importance of organization in effort and development of skill, and of the cost of tools and their need of care. He can be disciplined in these respects . . . but ordinarily he sees no reasons in this discipline; hence his 'forgetfulness,' his lapses, and his failures at crucial points" (Elizabeth Hoyt, "Economic Sense and the East African," *Africa*, 22:2, April 1952).

7 *Cf.* Daniel Lerner, *The Passing of Traditional Society* (New York, Free Press, 1958), for a portrait of the modernizing type of person. Also, *cf.* K. Ishwaran, *Tradition and Economy in Village India* (London, Routledge & Kegan Paul, 1966).

8 Everett Hagen has argued very persuasively that people on the margins of society are crucial for modernization. *Cf.* his *On the Theory of Social Change* (Homewood, Ill., Dorsey, 1962). Max Weber's classical position on the economic importance of "guest peoples" is also pertinent to this question.

9 *Cf.* Cyril Belshaw, *Traditional Exchange and Modern Markets* (Englewood Cliffs, N.J., Prentice-Hall, 1965). For an Indian case study, *cf.* Ishwaran, *op. cit.*

10 See Clifford Geertz's study of an Indonesian credit association in Immanuel Wallerstein (ed.), *Social Change* (New York, Wiley, 1966), pp. 420 ff.

11 As Geertz puts it (*loc. cit.*): "The degree to which, in any given case, the rotating credit association is an institution with *explicitly economic* aims and modes of operation is an index of the degree to which commercial motivations, attitudes and values have replaced diffusely social motivations, attitudes and values as controlling elements in the members' behavior within the economic context generally, the degree to which they have learned to discriminate between economic and 'non-economic' problems and processes and to act differentially with respect to them."

12 On political modernization generally, *cf.* Myron Weiner (ed.), *Modernization* (New York, Basic Books, 1966), Part III; Jason Finkle and Richard Gable (eds.), *Political Development and Social Change* (New York, Wiley, 1966).

13 Interesting data pertinent to this point in Africa may be found in Hunter, *op. cit., passim.*

14 *Cf.* Joseph LaPalombara and Myron Weiner (eds.), *Political Parties and Political Development* (Princeton, N.J., Princeton University Press, 1966); also, Finkle and Gable, *op. cit.* For case studies, *cf.*, for instance, Bhuwan Joshi and Leo Rose, *Democratic Innovations in Nepal* (Berkeley, University of California Press, 1966); Myron Weiner, *Party Building in a New Nation* (Chicago, University of Chicago Press, 1967); Lloyd Rudolph and Susanne Rudolph, *The Modernity of Tradition* (Chicago, University of Chicago Press, 1967); the last two studies both refer to India.

15 *Cf.* Ishwaran, *op. cit.* p. 119.

16 For a discussion of this from different viewpoints, *cf.* Peter Gutkind (ed.), *The Passing of Tribal Man in Africa* (Leiden, Brill, 1970).

17 *Cf.* Jean Duvignaud, *Change at Shebika* (New York, Pantheon, 1970).

18 *Cf.* W. F. Wertheim, *East-West Parallels* (Chicago, Quadrangle, 1965). A very instructive study of intellectuals in the modernizing situation, in India, is Edward Shils, *The Intellectual Between Tradition and Modernity* (The Hague, Mouton, 1961).

19 *Cf.* Julius Nyerere, *Ujamaa* (Dar es Salaam, Oxford University Press, 1968).

20 *Cf.* Paul Baran, *The Political Economy of Growth* (New York, Modern Reader Paperbacks, 1968); Andre Frank, *Capitalism and Underdevelopment in Latin America* (New York, Modern Reader Paperbacks, 1969); Armando Cordova and Hector Silva Michelena, *Aspectos teoricos del subdesarrollo* (Caracas, Universidad Central de Venezuela, 1967).

21 Lerner (*op. cit.*) has discussed this expansion of the social horizon under the categories of "empathy" and "mobility."

22 On "conscientization," *cf.* Paulo Freire, *Pedagogy of the Oppressed* (New York, Herder & Herder, 1970); on revolutionary consciousness, *cf.* Frantz Fanon, *The Wretched of the Earth* (New York, Grove, 1966).

23 *Cf.* J. P. Nettl, *Political Mobilization* (New York, Basic Books, 1967).

24 *Cf.* B. Goldenberg and K. Esser, *Zehn Jahre Kubanische Revolution* (Hannover, Verlag für Literatur und Zeitgeschichte, 1969); K.S. Karol, *Guerrillas in Power* (New York, Hill & Wang, 1970).

25 *Cf.* Lucian Pye's article on the military, in Finkle and Gable, *op. cit.*, pp. 379 ff. The importance of the military as a model for modernizing socialization is discussed in Marion Levy, *Modernization: Latecomers and Survivors* (New York, Basic Books, 1972).

26 The dichotomy of public and private spheres as an "ordeal," in the context of Jewish assimilation into Western societies, is discussed in John Murray Cuddihy, *Sigmund Freud's Ordeal of Civility* (Unpublished doctoral dissertation, Rutgers University, 1972).

CHAPTER 6

1 Jean Duvignaud, *Change at Shebika* (New York, Pantheon, 1970).

2 *Ibid.*, p. 207.

3 Daniel Lerner, *The Passing of Traditional Society* (New York, Free Press, 1958).

4 For an instructive study of an effort to cope ritually with the conflicts of modernization in everyday life, see James Peacock's study of folk theater in Indonesia, *Rites of Modernization* (Chicago, University of Chicago Press, 1968).

5 Duvignaud, *op. cit.*, p. 232.

6 *Cf.* Ivan Illich, *Deschooling Society* (New York, Harper & Row, 1971), for a very negative account of this process.

7 *Cf.* W. F. Wertheim, *East-West Parallels* (Chicago, Quadrangle, 1965), pp. 15 ff. We should also add that neither are we in a position to discuss the question of universal structures of consciousness as argued by Claude Lévi-Strauss and other "structuralists."

8 Jacques Binet, *Psychologie économique africaine* (Paris, Payot, 1970), p. 255. Our translation.

9 *Ibid.*, p. 258. Our translation.

10 John Mbiti, *African Religions and Philosophy* (Garden City, N.Y., Anchor, 1970), pp. 21 f.

11 William Hinton, *Fanshen* (New York, Vintage, 1966). In an appendix (pp. 623 ff), Hinton presents an official guide on "How to Analyze Class Status in the Countryside"—a handbook for the reclassification of social reality, as it were.

12 For a number of views on this, *cf.* Peter Gutkind (ed.), *The Passing of Tribal Man in Africa* (Leiden, Brill, 1970).

13 Colin Turnbull, *The Lonely African* (Garden City, N.Y., Anchor, 1963), pp. 162 ff.

14 Manning Nash, *Machine-Age Maya* (Chicago, Phoenix, 1967).

15 R. S. Khare, *The Changing Brahmans* (Chicago, University of Chicago Press, 1970). For the Hindu case, also *cf.* Lloyd Rudolph and Susanne Rudolph, *The Modernity of Tradition* (Chicago, University of Chicago Press, 1967).

16 Khare, *op. cit.*, pp. 184 ff.

17 *Ibid.*, p. 189.

18 *Cf.* Donald Smith (ed.), *Religion, Politics and Social Change in the Third World* (New York, Free Press, 1971), pp. 71 ff.

CHAPTER 7

1 *Cf.* Peter Worsley, *The Trumpet Shall Sound* (London, Mac-Gibbon and Kee, 1957).

2 *Cf.*, for example, Helio Jaguaribe *et al.*, *La dependencia polít-ico-economia de America Latina* (Mexico City, Siglo Veintiuno, 1970).

3 *Cf.* Charles Wilber, *The Soviet Model and Underdeveloped*

Countries (Chapel Hill, N.C., University of North Carolina Press, 1969).

4 *Cf.* Sylvia Thrupp (ed.), *Millennial Dreams in Action* (The Hague, Mouton, 1962); Vittorio Lanternari, *The Religion of the Oppressed* (New York, Knopf, 1963).

5 Lanternari, *op. cit.*, gives a concise account of this.

6 *Cf.* F. R. Wingate, *Mahdism and the Egyptian Sudan* (London, Cass, 1968).

7 *Cf.* Joan Bondurant and Margaret Fisher, "The Concept of Change in Hindu, Socialist and Neo-Gandhian Thought," in Donald Smith (ed.), *South Asian Politics and Religion* (Princeton, N.J., Princeton University Press, 1966), pp. 235 ff.

8 For a general discussion of this, in terms of the sociology of modern religion, *cf.* Peter Berger, *The Sacred Canopy* (Garden City, N.Y., Doubleday, 1967), Part II.

9 *Cf.*, for example, the articles by Yusif Sayigh and Noel Carlson in Robert Bellah (ed.), *Religion and Progress in Modern Asia* (New York, Free Press, 1965).

10 For all this, *cf.* Smith, *op. cit.*, as well as *Smith* (ed.), *Religion, Politics and Social Change in the Third World* (New York, Free Press, 1971).

11 For general discussions of this, *cf.* John Kautsky (ed.), *Political Change in Underdeveloped Countries* (New York, Wiley, 1962); Brigitte Berger, *Societies in Change* (New York, Basic Books, 1971), pp. 231 ff. For Asian cases, *cf.* F. W. Wertheim, *East-West Parallels* (Chicago, Quadrangle, 1965), pp. 85 ff.

12 For an African case study, *cf.* Brian Weinstein, *Gabon* (Cambridge, Mass., M.I.T. Press, 1966).

13 For a general discussion, *cf.* Brigitte Berger, *op. cit.*

14 *Cf.* John Kautsky, *Communism and the Politics of Development* (New York, Wiley, 1968).

15 Julius Nyerere, *Ujamaa* (Dar es Salaam, Oxford University Press, 1968), p. 12.

16 *Cf.* Ivan Illich, *Celebration of Awareness* (Garden City, N.Y., Anchor, 1971); Illich, *Deschooling Society* (New York, Harper & Row, 1971); also, the periodic publications of CIDOC, the institute founded by Illich in Cuernavaca, Mexico.

17 *Cf.* Paulo Freire, *Pedagogy of the Oppressed* (New York, Herder & Herder, 1970).

18 *Cf.*, for example, Rubem Alves, *A Theology of Human Hope* (New York, Corpus, 1969).

CHAPTER 8

1 *Cf.* Anton Zijderveld, *The Abstract Society* (Garden City, N.Y., Doubleday, 1970).

2 *Cf.* Peter Berger, *The Sacred Canopy* (Garden City, N.Y., Doubleday, 1967), Part II; Thomas Luckmann, *The Invisible Religion* (New York, Macmillan, 1967).

3 This term was coined by Arnold Gehlen. *Cf.* his *Die Seele im technischen Zeitalter* (Hamburg, Rowohlt, 1957).

4 This term, as well as the ensuing argument, are also taken from Gehlen.

5 *Cf.*, for example, the following study of modernization in Sicily, Johan Galtung, *Members of Two Worlds* (New York, Columbia University Press, 1971).

6 For a good summary of this position, *cf.* Daniel Bell, "The Post-Industrial Society," *Survey*, Spring 1971.

7 A major source for our view of this is Philippe Ariès, *Centuries of Childhood* (New York, Knopf, 1962).

8 F. Musgrove, *Youth and the Social Order* (Bloomington, Ind., Indiana University Press, 1965), p. 33.

9 Our view of these relationships is *not* to be confused with the neo-Freudian view—for example, that expressed by Lewis Feuer, *The Conflict of Generations* (New York, Basic Books, 1969). We think it quite erroneous to say that contemporary youth is rebelling against father figures. On the contrary, the rebellion is against the *absence* of paternal solicitude in the large bureaucratized structures. If anything, contemporary youth is *in search of* plausible father figures. The empirical evidence on the generally happy relations between campus rebels and their parents would seem to bear out our view—*cf.* Daniel Bell and Irving Kristol (eds.), *Confrontation* (New York, Basic Books, 1969).

10 A very instructive discussion of this may be found in an essay by Gehlen, provocatively entitled (our translation) "On the Birth of Freedom Out of Alienation," in *Studien zur Anthropologie und Soziologie* (Neuwied/Rhein, Luchterhand, 1963), pp. 232 ff. Also, *cf. id., Moral und Hypermoral* (Frankfurt, Athenäum, 1969).

11 By Luckmann, *op. cit.*

12 To translate this into the theoretical language of Talcott Parsons, modernity favors universalistic (as against particularistic) and ego-oriented (as against collectivity-oriented) patterns of social relations.

CHAPTER 9

1 In this chapter we revert to the method used in Part I of this book; that is, we try to describe certain structures of consciousness with which we have considerable firsthand experience. We have made no attempt to cover the current literature on the youth culture and the counterculture, much of which is journalistic and offers little reliable data. For an attempt to delineate the phenomenon of the youth culture, see the chapter "Youth" in Peter Berger and Brigitte Berger, *Sociology —A Biographical Approach* (New York, Basic Books, 1972). On the counterculture the two by now classical texts, Theodore Roszak's *The Making of a Counter-Culture* and Charles Reich's *The Greening of America* fall far short of giving a comprehensive analysis. Roszak's book (by far the more respectable intellectually) is a history-of-ideas discussion of a number of intellectual figures who have served as legitimations for the

counterculture; by its very procedure, the book fails to distinguish the legitimations from that which they serve to legitimate. Reich's book is the confession of a believing convert; it is useful as a compendium of ideological propositions, but not useful at all in analyzing them.

2 In this, at any rate, Reich's book is more perceptive than Roszak's: Reich's "Consciousness III" is clearly pre-theoretical.

3 *Cf.* Richard Neuhaus, *In Defense of People* (New York, Macmillan, 1971).

4 The German term *Übersehbarkeit* is appropriate here.

5 Anton Zijderveld has called this the current "anti-institutional mood."

6 There are interesting parallels to this in the history of religion. For example, ecstatic prophecy in the ancient Near East may well have manifested itself originally in disruptions of the priestly cult. At a later stage it was simply incorporated into it. Cult centers had priestly officers on their permanent staffs; the job of these officers was to supervise the ecstatic prophets and to integrate their potentially explosive performances into the official cult. It seems that they soon hit on the obvious idea of *scheduling* the ecstatic events—rather like saying, "Those possessed by god X will please limit their convulsive screams to the time between the first and second sacrifices." Eventually, as ecstasy became integrated with non-ecstatic operations, it became difficult to tell the two elements apart. Modern scholars of ancient cultic texts have come to detect the ecstatic component by certain linguistic forms—for instance, references to a divinity in the first person singular. Future scholars studying the minutes of meetings involving "programmed disruption" may have to use similar methods—perhaps by counting the frequency of obscene terms.

7 For those who prefer more conventional social-scientific concepts, we may add that our analysis of demodernization could also be put quite well in terms of Parsonian pattern variables. Thus: Demodernization entails a reversal in the modern trend from one set of pattern variables to the other. Demodernization seeks to move from universalism to particularism (for example, from abstract to concrete conceptions of rights); from performance to quality (denigration of the achievement ethos and reversal to ascriptive status); from functional specificity to functional diffuseness; from ego-orientation to collectivity-orientation; and, last but not least, from affective neutrality to affectivity. The reversal in the last three pairs of pattern variables, for instance, can be profitably studied in just about any youth-culture commune, with its values of rotating chores, relentless openness and all-embracing affection.

CHAPTER 10

1 We owe an empirical verification of this example to Richard Neuhaus. On a plane trip he described to a young fellow passenger, sitting next to him in full counterculture regalia, the alleged character of the "swinging airline" with which they were at that moment traveling—no

"uptight" regulations on staff discipline, pilots smoking pot and stewardesses putting out right in the cockpit, and so forth. All this, like, you
know, some 30,000 feet in the air. Needless to say, his companion went
into a state of barely controlled panic. The same example, incidentally,
could easily be translated into Third World terms. African airlines, for
instance, make a point of furnishing the passenger cabin in indigenous
décor, putting their stewardesses into African garb, and the like. But
they are equally eager to point out to the public that these manifestations of "African personality" do *not* extend to the technical operations
of actual aviation. We believe that even the most nationalistically minded
African politician (assuming he flies the national airline) finds reassur-
ance in this cultural "schizophrenia."

2 For the following argument on the relation of demodernization
to the class system, *cf.* Peter Berger and Brigitte Berger, "The Blueing
of America," *New Republic,* April 13, 1971.

3 The ethnic component of this scenario is beyond our scope here.
But it can be seen without much difficulty that the scenario is particularly negative in its implications for Wasps and Jews, and that its opportunity aspects are most relevant to other ethnic groups (including
blacks, to the extent that they do not come to be dominated by a demodernizing ethos of their own, which may define achievement in the
technological and bureaucratic structures of the larger society as some
sort of racial treason).

4 The ideas of Ivan Illich concerning educational "alternatives"
point toward such a pluralism.

5 Sociologists influenced by Emile Durkheim will assume that no
society can be viable without some common symbols that integrate all
its component groups in an overarching solidarity. They would further
assume that in the absence of such common symbols (that is, in our
terms, common cognitive and normative definitions of reality), the society would either fall apart or be held together by sheer coercive power.
One might hypothesize that these assumptions no longer hold in advanced industrial societies, which could operate on the basis of reciprocally negotiated pragmatic interests alone. We are inclined to believe
that the Durkheimian assumptions continue to hold.

6 It is for this reason, we believe, that the strongest response to
Illich's ideas on education has not come in Latin America (for which
these ideas were first developed), but in the United States.

Index

All three authors are sociologists.
PETER L. BERGER, professor of sociology
at Rutgers, is the author of many books,
including *Invitation to Sociology: The Social
Construction of Reality* (with Thomas Luckmann)
and *The Sacred Canopy*, which deals with the sociology
of religion. He is one of the editors of the magazine *Worldview*.

BRIGITTE BERGER teaches at Long Island University and is
the author of *Societies in Change*. She and Peter Berger have
collaborated on a textbook, *Sociology: A Biographical Approach*.

HANSFRIED KELLNER teaches at the University
of Darmstadt in West Germany.